Psychometric
Tests
FOR
DUMMIES®

Psychometric Tests FOR DUMMIES®

by Liam Healy

John Wiley & Sons, Ltd

Psychometric Tests For Dummies®
Published by
John Wiley & Sons, Ltd
The Atrium
Southern Gate
Chichester
West Sussex
PO19 8SQ
England

E-mail (for orders and customer service enquires): cs-books@wiley.co.uk

Visit our Home Page on www.wiley.com

For general information on our other products and services, please contact our Customer Care Department within the U.S. at 800-762-2974, outside the U.S. at 317-572-3993, or fax 317-572-4002.

For technical support, please visit www.wiley.com/techsupport.

Wiley also publishes its books in a variety of electronic formats. Some content that appears in print may not be available in electronic books.

British Library Cataloguing in Publication Data: A catalogue record for this book is available from the British Library

ISBN: 978-0-470-75366-8

Printed and bound in Great Britain by TJ International, Padstow, Cornwall

10

WILEY

About the Author

Liam Healy is a British Psychological Society registered Chartered Occupational Psychologist. He is a graduate of both Durham and Hull Universities where he won prizes for both his academic achievements and his research in Occupational Psychology. He is the Managing Director of www.CareerPsychologyCentre.com, a successful career guidance Web site, and is a senior consultant with Liam Healy & Associates.

Liam has been designing and using selection systems and psychometric tests for over a decade and is the author of several books and articles on the subject. He was one of the first people in the UK to design psychometric tests specifically for use on the Internet. He has helped hundreds of people prepare themselves for psychometric test sessions and carries out psychometric testing for corporate clients all over the world, both large and small.

Liam is also a software designer and programmer, and his research interests include the psychology of user behaviour on the Internet, human factors in software use, and guess what – psychometric test design. He lives on Tyneside with his family. You can visit him at www.psychometrics.co.uk and www.careerpsychologycentre.com.

Author's Acknowledgements

This was a technically complex and challenging book to write. Every question in this book was checked, re-checked, and checked again, but I didn't do it alone. A lot of people put in a lot of time to help me out. I need to thank Alan, Jane, Pat, Paul and his team, Lisa, Emma (for the loan of the junior encyclopaedia), Alex (for the loan of the toy cranes, trains, and bridges), and Steve and the team at Wiley who had no idea of the volume of work that awaited them. By now they have all seen so many tests that they need never fear a test again!

Finally, thanks to you, because no doubt you'll find any that we missed! If you do, well done – give yourself a pat on the back. With over a thousand practice questions, perhaps you can allow us one or two oversights!

Publisher's Acknowledgements

We're proud of this book; please send us your comments through our Dummies online registration form located at www.dummies.com/register/.

Some of the people who helped bring this book to market include the following:

Acquisitions, Editorial, and Media Development

Development Editor: Steve Edwards

Content Editor: Nicole Burnett

Copy Editor: Kate O'Leary

Proofreader: Andy Finch

Technical Editor: Dr Pat Lindley

Commissioning Editor: Wejdan Ismail

Publisher: Jason Dunne

Executive Project Editor: Daniel Mersey

Executive Editor: Samantha Spickernell

Cover Photos: Getty Images/ George Diebold

Cartoons: Ed McLachlan

Composition Services

Project Coordinator: Erin Smith

Layout and Graphics: Carl Byers, Alissa D. Ellet, Laura Pence

Proofreader: Laura Albert

Indexer: Cheryl Duksta

Special Help

Brand Reviewer: Rev Mengle

Contents at a Glance

Table of Contents

Introduction

● ●

*S*o you've bought a book called *Psychometric Tests For Dummies*. I bet you're feeling a bit worried! How do I know that, you may ask? Well, if you're preparing for a psychometric test but haven't ever faced one before, few things can seem as frightening. This book is ready to help. When you know a bit about them, you understand that psychometric tests are nothing to be afraid of.

What are psychometric tests, exactly? Psychometric tests are a series of standardised tasks that enable you to measure some aspect of your personality or ability. They are designed in such a way that everyone who takes them receives the same task to do and the same instructions for completing them. In most cases, this design allows the person administering the test to compare your performance to that of other people. Recruiters find this very helpful. After all, understanding the differences between candidates is their main goal.

Recruiting organisations use psychometric testing a lot during their selection processes, so you need to make sure that you're up to speed with it if you're in the job-hunting game. Candidates tend to share the same concerns about psychometric testing and look for answers to the same questions: How can I practise? How can I get better? What do I do if my results aren't what I expected? How do I stay calm?

I have designed, published, and administered psychometric tests to countless candidates over the years, and what I've written in this book is based on candidates' feedback to me about what they needed to know. I've written this book to take you through a few practice tests, dispel a few anxiety-provoking myths, let you in on a few tips and tricks (including how to spot an unqualified test user who doesn't know what he or she is doing), and hopefully help to demystify the whole subject for you. Most people do just fine on psychometric tests, and you can probably do better on psychometric tests than you think, but a little help never goes amiss.

So please read on, and see if psychometric testing is as frightening as you think! I hope that you're pleasantly surprised, and reassured by how knowing a bit about the subject can help keep you calm and relaxed. And a relaxed you is sure to do much better on a test than a stressed you!

Seriously, though, well done for picking up this book and looking to do some constructive preparation. If you want to make a success of your psychometric tests, this book is the one for you.

Finally, this book has lots of practice tests. Do as many as you can. Familiarise yourself with their layout, what they expect of you, and how you'll be appraised. Knowing what you're going to face on the day may not conquer your nerves, but it does make you more confident.

About This Book

My aim is to help you prepare for a psychometric test session. As well as explaining *intellectual ability* and *personality*, and how they are measured, I help you to develop your understanding of what psychometric tests are by explaining why and how recruiters use them. I give you lots of opportunity to try some of the more common practice tests:

- ✔ **Verbal ability tests** (spelling, grammar, comprehension, and critical thinking)
- ✔ **Numerical ability tests** (mathematical ability and higher-level numerical reasoning)
- ✔ **Abstract reasoning tests** (including creative and strategic thinking)
- ✔ **Technical ability tests** (including mechanical, spatial, and detail/accuracy tests)

You can also try out a personality test and even draw up a rough personality profile for yourself. In all, this book has a couple of dozen sample tests and over one thousand individual test questions. Plenty to keep you busy!

I also cover two vital but often overlooked areas – how to prepare yourself for your psychometric test session and how to deal with the post-test feedback. I also look at dealing with

Internet-based tests, and what to do if your test results aren't as good as you hoped for. Much of the advice is based on what candidates have said to me. So I not only tell you what I think is important as a test user, but also what previous candidates, just like you, have told me they need to know.

I've designed the book so that you can start reading anywhere you want to. You don't need to read this book in sequence. You can start at the beginning and work your way through, but if you're under time pressure you can go straight to Part III and get started on the sample tests. I recommend that you avoid reading the answers first, though! You can skip the sidebars (the grey boxes) without missing anything crucial, though you may find them fun to read.

This book is yours, and I want you to use it to suit your own needs. I designed this book for you to interact with, and so feel free to scribble, doodle, draw, write, jot, and tick all over it. Do sums in the margins and check your spelling on the front cover!

Conventions Used in This Book

To make the text more readable, this book often uses different words interchangeably to mean the same thing. For example, the words *recruiter*, *selector*, and *test user* all mean the same thing – the person who carries out the test. I specifically use the term *interviewer* to refer to the person who carries out the feedback interview with you.

I use the terms *ability*, *intellectual ability*, and *aptitude* to mean the same thing – intelligence. I sometimes use the word *reasoning* in front of *ability* when I describe a higher level of ability. *Personality* and *character* also mean the same thing, and *test items* are the same thing as *test questions*.

To help you identify Web addresses, they're printed in `mono-font`. In Web addresses that run onto a second line of text, rest assured that I haven't put in any extra characters (such as hyphens) to indicate the break. So, when using one of these Web addresses, just type in exactly what you see in this book, as though the line break doesn't exist.

I use *italic* for emphasis, and to highlight any new words or terms that are defined.

Foolish Assumptions

I know that few people buy books on psychometric testing for a bit of light bedtime reading, and so I've made a few assumptions about you:

- ✔ You're due to face a psychometric test, or think you may be facing one soon, and want to know what to expect and how to give yourself the best possible chance of success. Therefore, this book contains illustrations of the most common types of test – not every single one you may come across!

- ✔ You have a basic grasp of English and maths.

- ✔ You're looking to be stretched a bit, and want to improve your skills at taking a test.

- ✔ You're probably more interested in dealing with the practicalities of sitting a psychometric test than in the theory behind testing. You want to know enough and have advice and resources to hand that enable you to improve and make the most of your abilities.

- ✔ You're due to take a test rather than to administer one! The tests in this book are designed to help you improve your skills in preparation for a test. They aren't to be used in real-life recruitment situations or by unqualified test users. So, if you are a recruiter, as opposed to a candidate, and wondering whether the tests can be used in real life selection, the answer is 'no'!

How This Book Is Organised

I've divided this book into four parts, and broken each part into chapters. Part III contains the actual tests, and Parts I, II, and IV deal with other issues to do with the testing process.

Part 1: Testing Basics

Part I looks at what psychometric tests are and how they are used in recruitment and selection. This part also covers some important aspects of how best to prepare for a psychometric test session, why tests are used, how the results are interpreted, and how to deal with post-test feedback. Psychometric testing can be stressful, no one is denying that, but the advice in this part can help make your testing day go as smoothly and be as stress-free as possible.

Part II: Finding Out About Different Types of Tests

Part II looks at the abilities and characteristics that tests are used to measure. I cover the nature of verbal ability, numerical ability, abstract ability, technical ability, and personality, and I describe how tests are used to measure these aspects. This part also includes advice about how to deal with specific types of test. From each section in this part you can jump straight to the relevant full-length test in Part III.

Part III: Getting Some Practise In: Sample Tests

Part III is where you find all the full-length tests that are touched on in Part II. Each test described in Part II has its own full version in Part III so you can skip straight to it. The answers follow immediately after each test. I try to prepare you for the most common styles of test that you're likely to come across, and even if the test you ultimately face is in a slightly different format, the same underlying abilities are being measured.

Part IV: The Part of Tens

Part IV is a useful compendium of tips, and is probably the final thing to read just before you're tested. The content in this part is all about you, and not about tests. I look at ten things to remember to do during the test session and ten ways to stay calm! You may even find it useful to read this part of the book first.

Icons Used in This Book

I use a number of different icons throughout this book to help you locate particular kinds of information.

This icon highlights practical suggestions that you may find useful.

This icon reminds you of points I've covered earlier, but that are relevant to the current section.

Watch for this icon; it draws your attention to things to take note of, and mistakes to avoid!

Psychometric testing is based on a lot of theory and statistics. You don't need to worry about them too much, but if you're interested I use this icon to describe some of the technical aspects of what's going on behind all the practical stuff.

Where to Go from Here

You don't have to read this book from cover to cover. You can just dip into the bits that are most relevant to you, but digesting most of what's in the book is probably a good idea. You can find a lot of good advice in this book outside of the practise test chapters.

Of course, your story doesn't end with your test results – it only starts there. Wanting to take stock of where you are with your career after going through the testing process is natural. Irrespective of whether it's been successful or not, many people find the testing process to be an enlightening one. You can look in more detail at what to do after you receive your results in Chapter 4. In addition, you can go to my dedicated career-support Web site at www.careerpsychologycentre. com for some free career support resources and general information about developing your career.

If you want to develop your basic verbal and numerical skills even further, and explore the answers to the tests in this book in a bit more detail, visit my Web site at www.psychometrics. co.uk/dummies.htm. (This page is private and just for my *Dummies* friends, so if you haven't read this book you won't know about it – ssshh!)

Based on what candidates tell me, you're likely to be lying in bed the night before a test reading this! If you are, read Chapter 16 before you drift off: It helps you get a good night's sleep.

Finally, if you're being tested tomorrow, I wish you success, not only in your test, but also in your future life and career.

It's not *all* about work, you know.

Part I
Testing Basics

'Pretty confident aren't you, Mr. Tollboothe.'

In this part . . .

This part covers everything you need to know about what psychometric tests are, what they're designed to measure, how and why they're used, and ways to prepare yourself for a test session.

I also cover one of the most important but often overlooked aspects of testing – dealing with feedback and understanding what your scores actually mean.

Chapter 1

Understanding Psychometric Tests

- -

In This Chapter

▶ Looking at what tests measure

▶ Distinguishing the range of different tests available

▶ Understanding the differences between personality and intelligence tests

▶ Seeing how tests are used in practice

- -

*P*sychometric tests are a series of standardised tasks, designed in such a way that everyone who takes them receives the same task to do and the same instructions for doing them. Two main types of test exist: tests that have right or wrong answers, and tests in which you say what's typical of you. The first group are called *intelligence* or *ability tests* and the second group include *personality* or *vocational interest questionnaires* or *tests*.

You can be forgiven for thinking that a test is just a list of questions that somebody decided to write one day. Well, there's a little more to testing than that, as you find out in this book!

In this chapter I explain how psychometric tests are designed to measure the two things about you that recruiters are most interested in – intelligence and personality – and how the tests are designed to be as fair as possible. I also explain the different types of test that recruiters use, how those tests are used in practice, and where they fit into the whole recruitment process. I also explode a few myths about testing, just to help put you at ease!

Where does testing come from?

People have always wanted to know what goes on inside other people's heads. The first scientific-*ish* attempts to work this out were made by Hippocrates in the fourth century BC. He thought that different bodily fluids, or *humours*, could explain human personality. According to Hippocrates, cheerful or sanguine people were characterised by *blood*, dominant and impatient people were characterised by yellow bile, creative people were characterised by *black bile*, and those characterised by *phlegm* tended to be placid and relaxed. The nineteenth century witnessed the first modern attempt to understand what human characteristics (specifically intelligence) were and how they could be measured when Francis Galton looked at reaction time as an indicator of intelligence. In the early 1900s Alfred Binet developed the idea that you can measure intelligence indirectly through *behaviour*. Binet began to measure things like numerical and verbal skills and introduced the idea of having different *difficulty levels* in a

test. This idea meant that tests could be pitched at the appropriate level for the group of people whose abilities you were measuring.

Even today, the use of testing (particularly *intelligence* or *ability testing*) is not without controversy. Many psychologists acknowledge that differences that seem to exist in test scores across gender and race are more to do with cultural, social, and educational influences, and errors in the testing process, than anything else.

History provides several examples of how researchers prodded and poked the brains of live subjects (both human and animal) to explore the brain. A depressing thought is that much of what we know today about the brain and its relationship to thought and behaviour comes from studies like these. At least we can be thankful that we've moved on from the days of Hippocrates, and that you're unlikely to be asked for samples of bodily fluids prior to an interview!

Identifying What Tests Measure

The word *psychometric* comes from *psycho* meaning mental, and *metric* meaning measurement.

The problem with measuring *anything* that goes on inside your head is exactly that – it's *inside* your head – and recruiters are faced with the tricky problem of never being able to observe *directly* the very things they're interested in.

So, they tend to focus more on the outcome of what goes on inside your head (that is, your *behaviour*) or your performance in a test.

Understanding intelligence and ability tests

What you are *capable* of doing is determined by your intelligence, but what actually is *intelligence*? Many psychologists think of intelligence as being either *crystallised* (that is, acquired skills and knowledge) or *fluid* (flexible reasoning ability). General intelligence or *general ability* is also made up of a series of *aptitudes* or *specific abilities* – verbal ability, numerical ability, abstract ability (sometimes known as creative or strategic ability), and technical ability (which includes spatial and mechanical ability).

A numerical ability test that presented you with questions you'd never seen before would be measuring how you apply your specific crystallised numerical knowledge in a fluid way. In practical terms, almost all ability tests look at your level of *fluid intelligence*. Ability tests contain sets of questions organised around measuring specific individual abilities, such as verbal, numerical, technical, and abstract ability. If a recruiter is only interested in a single aspect of your intelligence such as your verbal ability, you may be asked only to complete a verbal ability test. If, on the other hand, she's interested in your overall level of intelligence or *ability*, you may be asked to complete a range of different ability tests to give an overall picture of your intellectual ability.

The key feature of ability tests is that they have right and wrong answers, and the score you obtain is a judgemental measure of your intellectual ability.

When you hear psychometric test boffins using terms such as ability, intellectual ability, aptitude, or intelligence, they are talking about the same thing.

Understanding personality tests

Your *personality* is crucial in determining how well you can apply your intellectual ability to the real world. Different theories exist about what exactly personality is (you won't be surprised to hear that not everyone agrees on which theory is the correct one). These theories range from Freud's idea that personality is driven by unconscious motives, through to Maslow's notion that people are driven to satisfy needs. *Type* theories suggest that you can classify people according to a number of finite *personality types*. Type measurements are mostly used in training and development, because the way your type is calculated makes comparing candidates against each other in a recruitment setting rather difficult.

The idea that personality is made up of five main *traits* (the 'Big Five' theory) is perhaps the most widely accepted and useful theory for recruiters. This theory breaks down each main trait into a number of more specific traits. Table 1-1 shows you these main traits.

Table 1-1   The Five Main Personality Traits

Personality Trait	Behaviours Associated with a High Trait Score	Behaviours Associated with a Low Trait Score
Extraversion	Externally focused, outgoing	Internally focused, reflective
Stability	High self-esteem, calm, relaxed	Low self-esteem, anxious, worrying
Thinking style	Task focused, logical, mechanical	Sensitive, creative, strategic
Independence	Assertive, confident	Submissive, shy
Conscientiousness	Rule governed, structured, self-disciplined	Disorganised, unstructured

Personality tests measure how much a person has of these traits and then compare candidates against each other. Each trait represents a *continuum* with certain behaviours at one end, and 'opposite' behaviours at the other, so the idea of a 'good' score or 'pass mark' on a personality test makes no sense. Seeing how candidates with very different personalities can all bring something unique to a job is always a pleasure.

How your personality can hinder – or help – your ability

I once carried out an assessment for a customer service manager role. The candidate had a high level of numerical reasoning ability and easily dealt with the complexities of customer accounts. However, she wasn't very assertive, and found dealing with customers difficult. So although she was able to perform tasks to a high standard, her personality limited her ability to do the job in a live situation. Clearly, this person was better suited to a job where she could apply her talents, without having to challenge others.

This principle also works in the other direction – if a person is well organised and motivated, she can often apply a somewhat limited level of ability to great effect.

The key feature of personality tests is that they have no right or wrong answers, and the score you obtain is a description of, rather than a judgement about, your personality. Technically, a personality test is not a *test* at all – because you can't 'pass' or 'fail' – but more a descriptive questionnaire. For convenience most people still refer to them as tests, and I retain that convention here.

Working Fast, Working Hard: Speed Tests versus Power Tests

Two common styles of ability test are regularly used – speed and power tests. They both measure your ability, but do so in different ways. This distinction doesn't apply in personality tests.

Speed tests – smarties fast!

Speed tests are often used for lower-level jobs. Speed tests ask you to complete a large number of quite easy questions, are strictly timed, (commonly lasting around 25 minutes), and can comprise anything up to 60 or more questions.

The key with these tests is to hit the ground running and work fast!

Power tests – intellectual muscle

You're more likely to come across *power tests* for higher-level jobs. Power tests ask you a smaller number of much harder questions, each comprising some information followed by four or five related questions. These tests are more concerned with the *quality* of your performance.

Power tests often have generous time limits, because you're meant to take time arriving at the correct answer. Any time limit that does apply is often quite long (maybe an hour or more), and is based on the principle that if you haven't worked out the right answers by then, you never will! The key here is to fully digest the information presented first. Don't rush in and start answering questions straight away. Power tests are about quality rather than speed.

Make sure that you understand the nature of any time limit you're given for a test, and whether that limit is fixed or just given to you as a guide.

Seeing How Tests Are Used in Practice

These days you may easily think that everyone uses psychometric tests! Historically, tests tended to be the sole preserve of Human Resources (HR) staff, but nowadays you're just as likely to find testing being used by a non-HR manager within a company. Test results are often considered by a wider range of people than just the HR department to ensure that the company recruits the right person for the job.

Preparing to recruit

Before initiating any tests, a recruiting organisation needs to produce two documents:

- ✔ **Job description.** The recruiter prepares the job description by carrying out a systematic job analysis. This analysis identifies the key tasks required in the job in question.

- ✔ **Person specification.** This document stipulates what characteristics a candidate needs in order to do the tasks described in the job description. The whole recruitment process is geared towards assessing the characteristics listed in the person specification. Without it, the choice of any selection tool is little more than random. When a client asks me, 'Can you come and do some personality assessments for us?', I always ask to see the person specification first, so I can decide whether a personality test is the right way forward.

When the person specification is written, the recruiter can decide on the most appropriate test or other assessment method. Often, an interview, presentation, or other form of activity may be chosen in preference to a test. The key point is that tests aren't just used for the sake of it when a better alternative selection tool exists.

How tests are administered

Each test has a set of administration instructions that should cover some example questions, test-specific instructions on how to make your responses, and time limits.

Testing, testing . . .

Although you may think otherwise, test design is anything but arbitrary. Modern *psychometricians* (yes, that's the catchy title we go by!) are more statistician than psychologist. Test design involves a complex statistical process to ensure that a test is accurate, fair, and focuses only on the things that the test is designed to measure. Tests are constructed using an accepted set of rules and a good quality test can take many years and several thousand trial subjects to produce. Many tests never get published because they fail to meet the stringent standards required. Unfortunately, test publication and use is not legally regulated in the UK so not all tests live up to these high standards. Hundreds of tests are in use today in the UK, although a core of around 20–30 are used most often.

When the test starts you are under exam conditions, and aren't normally allowed to ask further questions. Make sure that you pay close attention to the instructions and make full use of the opportunity to ask questions before the test starts.

With an Internet-based test you may not be able to ask questions as you would during a face-to-face session. Online tests should have a help system for recording any problems that may have affected your performance. Otherwise, make a mental note of any issues and e-mail these to the recruiting organisation when the test is over.

Skip over to Chapter 2 for more information about test administration.

How tests are scored and interpreted

With most tests, your score is compared to the scores obtained by a reference or *norm* group, so the recruiter can put your score into a meaningful context and compare your performance to that of the other people of known ability. This is why no such thing as a 'pass mark' in tests exists.

Choosing the right norm group for an ability test is crucial. Choosing a norm group based on school leavers for a test of graduate-level ability would be pointless – all the candidates would seem to do brilliantly!

With personality tests, the recruiter uses the score to place you (the candidate) somewhere along a personality trait scale (for example, an *assertiveness scale*) so she can say whether you're more assertive than average, less assertive than average, or about the same as most people. Personality assessment is descriptive rather than judgemental, so personality test scores are often compared to a reference group based on the adult population.

Your score is most commonly described in terms of *A to E grades*, or *percentiles*. Other more technical scoring scales, such as *T-scores, Z-scores, stens,* or *stanines* are sometimes used. You don't need to understand the fine detail of these systems, but it is important to understand that they all do the same thing – allow the recruiter to know where your score falls in relation to the comparison group average. If the recruiter knows what she's doing, she should take some time during feedback to explain the scoring system she has used. (See Chapter 4 for more on dealing with feedback.)

Predicting the future – did the test get it right?

The key thing that the recruiter is interested in afterwards is assessing how well the test predicted work performance. After all, that's the whole point of using a test!

Recruiters sometimes use a large-scale statistical study to quantitatively examine the relationship between test scores and work performance. Alternatively, a team of experts on the job in question may simply consider how well the test predicted work performance. This qualitative method tends to be used when smaller numbers of candidates apply for the job, or if the job is very specialist and conducting large-scale statistical analysis just isn't feasible.

Distinguishing Test Myth from Test Fact

A few myths have developed around psychometric tests. Table 1-2 shows a few of the more common ones, plus a few words on the reality.

Table 1-2	Testing Fiction and Fact
Testing Fiction	*Testing Fact*
Psychometric tests have a pass mark.	Wrong. The highest scoring candidates are usually viewed more favourably. Personality tests *never* have a pass mark.
A poor ability test score means you are stupid.	No. A poor ability test score just means you didn't score highly on that particular test. You may find dealing with complex problems relying on the type of ability the test measures more difficult.

(continued)

Table 1-2 (continued)

Testing Fiction	Testing Fact
Tests are unfair.	Wrong. If they're well designed and used properly, tests are one of the fairest selection methods.
Tests have trick questions to catch you out.	No, they don't. Good tests are fair and accurate measures.
In a personality test you need to tell the recruiters what they want to hear.	Wrong. You need to tell them the truth. If you get a job based on a less than honest description of yourself on a personality test, you probably won't be too happy. Your personality and the job may not match up that well.
You can 'trick' a test.	Wrong. You can't trick an ability test – if you don't know the correct answer you can't fool the test into thinking you do. Misrepresenting yourself in a personality test is possible, but you may get found out during the feedback session.
I'm just no good at tests.	You're probably better than you think. Your performance improves with practice.
Tests are designed to be impossible to complete.	No, but tests are designed to stretch you – recruiters want to see how *well* you can do, not how poorly.
Anyone can write a test.	Perhaps, but the test may not be much good. Good tests take considerable expertise and many years to develop.
You need to revise for a test.	No, you don't. Ability tests don't rely on knowledge. You can prepare yourself in other ways. Personality tests require no preparation at all.
Recruiters use tests because they like to see candidates suffer!	The opposite is true! Recruiters want to give candidates a favourable opinion of their company – after all, they want the candidate to work there.

Chapter 2

Setting Your Mind at Rest About Psychometric Tests

*Y*ou have little to fear from a well-known and properly administered test, with clear, well thought-out reasons for its use. Most people's hair stands on end when they think they're going to be tested, but psychometric tests are your best guarantee of fairness and keep your fellow candidates on a level playing field with you.

Don't get too upset about all this objectivity. A planned, evidence-based approach to recruitment, using tools that have been shown to assess those characteristics required in a job, is the fairest way of doing things. In any other aspect of life you'd be positively livid if you paid a professional to do a job and he failed to carry out a systematic, thorough, and objective assessment of your condition. Imagine how you'd feel if your dentist failed to check whether you really did need that filling before starting up the drill!

Although you may feel more comfortable in an old-fashioned, freewheeling interview, you're at your most vulnerable because of the possible biases and stereotypical views of the interviewer. Give me a test over an interview any day of the week.

In this chapter I describe the difference between a good test and a bad test, and consider why recruiters use psychometric tests so much. I also explain how tests are designed to be as fair as possible. You leave this chapter knowing why some form of testing is often inevitable, and able to appreciate that psychometric testing done well isn't the evil it's often cracked up to be, but can actually work for you.

Knowing What Tests Can Tell Recruiters About You

Face it – sometimes you *have* to feel sorry for recruiters. They have an impossible job. On the one hand, they know that perfect candidates don't exist (that's why companies have training and development programmes!). On the other hand, they have to work out a way of choosing from the imperfect candidates in front of them who they're going to offer a job to.

Recruiters are under pressure to get their decision right, and are usually appointing on behalf of a manager. They expect that manager to give them some *serious* grief if they get their decision wrong, so you can see why recruiters sometimes assess candidates to within an inch of their life!

Recruiters want to see the *real* you; the you who'll have to deal with their biggest client screaming down the phone that he's taking his business elsewhere because an order hasn't arrived on time.

Ask yourself: *If I were in their shoes, what would I do?*

First, you'd want an assessment method to be objective and free from bias. Second, you'd want to be able to compare your candidates with each other, and possibly with your current employees.

Psychometric tests are one of the best ways for the recruiter to gain an accurate picture of your strengths and weaknesses, and to see how you compare with the other candidates. Tests can be very accurate and allow the recruiter to focus in on very specific attributes. For example, a recruiter may use a test in order to answer questions about how good person is at a specific ability, such as verbal or numerical reasoning, or how assertive, socially confident, or able to deal with pressure a candidate is compared to other people.

Selecting a candidate for a job is always a gamble because a test can never predict with 100 per cent accuracy how a person is going to perform in a job. But using a test enables recruiters to know that they are at least picking people who've shown they have the necessary skills and characteristics needed to give them the best chance of doing the job well.

Viewing the Process Positively

Any selection decision must be based purely on the ability to do the job. Irrelevant information must not be considered. I'm amazed that in this day and age I still come across recruiters who say something along the lines of, 'Hmm, I don't know, there's something I don't like about this candidate, my gut instinct tells me something's not quite right.'

I always challenge this 'gut instinct' rubbish when I hear it. If a required characteristic is not being explicitly identified and measured, I insist that we go back to reviewing the job analysis, job description, person specification, and the assessment tools we use. No areas should be missed, and nothing should be left to 'gut instinct'.

I have asked more than one client, 'If you bumped into this candidate in the pub tonight and he cornered you about why he didn't get the job – could you justify your decision?' Fortunately, not hiring someone simply because the recruiter doesn't like the 'look' of him is illegal. If recruiters are influenced in this way, and manage to get away with it, more fool them – I can't think of a better way to miss out on excellent candidates.

 Any company who wants to hire people based on 'gut instinct' may well run the rest of its business like a popularity contest as well – and so you probably don't want to work there anyway.

Tests are one of the best ways of ensuring fairness, and provide a logical, reliable alternative to hiring employees using some supposed sixth sense.

Knowing What Makes a Good Test

Good psychometric tests have certain obvious features:

- ✔ The test is presented in a high quality 'professional' format – properly printed, if it's a traditional pencil and paper-type, or on a well-devised and constructed Web site or computer program.

- ✔ The test and the accompanying detailed instructions are written to a high standard, with no obvious grammar or spelling mistakes – unless of course it's measuring your ability to spot them! Test instructions, though, should never contain any grammar or spelling mistakes.

- ✔ Before beginning the test, you're given some practice questions to help you understand how the questions are to be put to you, and to make sure that you're marking your answers in the correct way. You're normally also given the answers to these practice questions.

- ✔ You have an opportunity to ask questions, which you can take if you don't understand the answers to the practice questions.

- ✔ The test bears a copyright notice and the publisher's name.

- ✔ The test instructions make clear that the administrator can't usually enter into discussions about individual questions while the test is underway.

- ✔ The test is reliable, consistent, and valid. In other words, the test actually measures what it's supposed to measure and doesn't include anything inessential. These elements are calculated statistically before the test is published to determine the structure and question content of the test.

- ✔ The test is long enough to build up a representative picture of your abilities or personality over a range of situations.

Much of the test development process involves identifying and disposing of test questions that discriminate between people on irrelevant factors such as age, ethnicity, and gender. This (hopefully!) results in a test that only discriminates between people on the ability in question.

Recognising and Dealing With Dodgy Tests

Unfortunately, the psychometric testing market isn't legally regulated. Unqualified people can write a poor quality test and supply it for use in a totally unrestricted manner. The increasing use of the Internet as an administration medium hasn't really helped the situation.

Some theories of personality can produce appealing 'tests' that unfortunately lack the careful development and interpretation that psychometric tests should have. The best known of these theories is Freud's *Psychoanalytic Theory of Personality* (bet *that* surprised you – after all, it was Freud's theory that spawned the word 'Ego'). Freud's theory revolves around the *unconscious mind*, of which by definition the person is unaware, and so it's very difficult to observe and relies on highly skilled administration and interpretation. In addition, some of the content of Freud's theory can be described as pretty personal!

Be on your guard if you're faced with any of the following:

✔ A personality test that asks you to provide a sample of handwriting for analysis. As with Freudian 'tests', you can have a result and a report that is slick but without any underpinning development to support it.

✔ A personality test that asks you about sexual or violent motives (Freudian).

✔ A personality test that shows you pictures or scenarios and asks you to place interpretations on the actors' motives, or say what you think an abstract figure resembles (Freudian).

✔ A personality test that asks you to say which word comes into your head when presented with another (Freudian).

The problem with IQ

IQ is simply a way of saying how a child's intellectual ability compares to that of other children of the same age. Once you reach early adulthood, the idea of IQ becomes meaningless, because your mental age eventually aligns with your chronological age.

The measurement of IQ has no place in occupational selection.

If you come across a test that you're uncomfortable with, do remember that you're not obliged to complete it. However, refusing to do so probably rules you out of the selection process. Unless you find the content to be very personal, intrusive, or upsetting, completing the assessment may be the best way forward. However, make sure that the rationale for using the test, and the results, are explained to you during feedback.

Sussing Out Your Administrator

You usually find one test *administrator* to every 6–12 candidates. A single administrator may find it difficult to supervise larger groups of candidates and deal with any unexpected events that arise. A test administrator, although trained in test administration, doesn't have to be trained to the same standard as the test *user*, who needs to know how to choose a test and interpret the results. You may not always be in a position to spot the signs, but the proficient administrator who fully understands the testing procedure:

- ✔ Adheres to the administration instructions

- ✔ Allows you to go through the practice examples again if you don't understand them first time around

- ✔ Assists with instructions and administration when required (some tests *are* designed to be self-administering, but most pencil and paper versions require at least some input from the administrator)

- ✔ Encourages you to ask questions

✔ Is confident

✔ Is familiar with the administration instructions

✔ Understands why the correct answers to the practice examples *are* the correct answers

Online tests should give you detailed interactive instructions in a step-by-step sequence that checks you understand each section before asking you to move onto the next. Online test administration should have at least two important features: First, it shouldn't commit you to starting the actual test until you're ready to do so; Second, it allows you to cycle freely back and forth through the instructions so that you can study the examples and directions until you're happy you understand everything.

Some online tests may formally require you to tick a box before you begin the test to confirm that you understand what you have to do and how you have to do it.

Tests look very easy to administer and interpret to the untrained eye. Poor administration renders a 'good' test useless. Administrators know that candidates can perform poorly on a test just because they didn't understand the instructions, so they take extra care to make sure that all the candidates understand what is expected of them.

Each test has a set of administration instructions to ensure that each candidate sits the test under similar conditions. Ability tests in particular are strictly supervised. The administration should provide you with time limits, example questions to help get you going, and some test-specific instructions on how to answer the questions.

Receiving the right instructions

If, when a test is developed, trial volunteers are given the instruction 'Work as quickly as you can', but the people being tested later on in a 'live' situation are instructed to 'Work as carefully as you can', the two groups may perform quite differently. This discrepancy would make fair comparisons between the two groups difficult – and all because someone was sloppy with the administration instructions.

Administrators are at their happiest when everyone knows what they're supposed to be doing, so you can ask questions without feeling embarrassed. I've seen too many candidates perform poorly on a test because they thought that asking for clarification would reflect badly on them.

You're under exam conditions when the test begins, and aren't usually allowed to ask any more questions from that point. So closely reading the instructions and asking questions before the test begins is important.

Questions to do with why the organisation is using this particular test, or queries to do with how the test is administered, scored and interpreted, are a bit too detailed to ask before the test, so deal with these issues during your feedback session (Chapter 4 covers receiving feedback).

Administration instructions can take up to a third of the total time allotted for a test. Pay close attention to these instructions and use that time well. Asking questions shows the administrator that you have engaged with the process.

Any time limits set on a test are very real, and strictly adhered to. You aren't allowed any more time than the other candidates just because you need to leave to go to the toilet. I always use two stopwatches and start and check them in full view of the candidates, to emphasise just how seriously strict timing is taken.

Chapter 3

Preparing For a Psychometric Test

*W*hen you're anxious during a test you may perform well below par. Your objective with ability tests is to perform as closely to your maximum level of ability as possible. Your objective with personality tests is to answer the questions in a way that reflects the real 'you' (not the 'stressed out' you!). This chapter helps you to keep anxiety at bay and stay calm, so that on the day of the test all you need to worry about is the test itself – and hopefully, not even worry about that too much!

In the run up to the test session you need to remove as many sources of stress as you can. Feeling *well organised* and *in control* is the key.

In this chapter I talk primarily about the preparations you need to make for a face-to-face test session, and I also deal with the specifics of preparing for an Internet-based test session.

Getting Yourself Ready

Effective planning is essential, so that by the morning of the test you have little to do other than turn up and complete the test.

Here are a few tasks you can do in the week before your test to get your preparation going.

✔ **Make a list of the preparation you need to do for the test, and keep it updated.** Refer to this *action list* regularly and tick things off as you do them.

✔ **Arrange any childcare you may need.**

✔ **Arrange time off work, if necessary.** Taking a day off is better than lying and saying you have a dentist appointment! You don't want to have to deal with the stress and fear of being caught out.

✔ **Identify any day-to-day hassles you need to get out of the way.** Does your car need an MOT? Do you have a pile of washing and ironing to do? Get them sorted now.

✔ **Make sure that you know where the test session is being held and plan your travel arrangements.** Get a map or directions – and check that these are understandable!

  • **If you're driving to the test session, make sure that you know the parking arrangements.**

  • **If you're travelling by train, find out who books and pays for the tickets – you or the company?** Have a standby travel plan in case the train gets delayed or cancelled.

✔ **Check the access requirements.** Do you need a visitors' pass and how is that arranged? Where do you report once you arrive: reception, an office, or a training room?

✔ **Find out if refreshments are provided on the day or if you need to provide your own.**

✔ **If you have a timetable involving other assessment activities, study it and prepare for any other tasks you may face (for example, a presentation), well in advance.**

✔ **Make sure that you receive any available practice test examples** and begin to work through any that the organisation may have provided for you, as well as the relevant examples in this book. Ask someone to administer the test to you, complete with stopwatch and stern voice to prepare you for the actual session!

✔ **Choose a time of day to practise when you're at your most alert.** Practise every day, but don't overdo it – take regular breaks and maintain a sense of perspective; they're only tests.

✔ **If you have any medical or other condition, or take any medication, which may affect your performance on the day, ask your doctor for advice.**

✔ **Let the organisation know about any special requirements you may have.**

On the day before the test:

✔ **Don't get up too late.** Lying in may stop you getting to sleep that night.

✔ **Keep yourself busy and your mind active, so that you feel tired enough to sleep that evening.**

✔ **Go over your travel plans.** Double-check the details.

✔ **If you're driving, check whether you have enough petrol in your car.**

✔ **Check whether the organisation needs you to confirm that you're still attending the test session, and do so if required.**

✔ **Try some practice tests again, but don't spend too long on them.**

On the night before your test:

✔ **Get all your clothes and toiletries ready to go for the next morning.** The organisation should tell you whether it has any dress code; if none is mentioned, there's no harm in checking. Generally though, unless you've been told otherwise, dress formally and smartly. Some organisations may tell you how to dress, and with good reason – wearing a tie or jewellery can contravene health and safety rules if your recruitment session involves a tour of a manufacturing or production site. Similarly, if you're facing a practical work sample test (for example, a welding test or food-handling test), specialist attire may well be needed, and be provided for you.

✔ **Make sure that you have at least two pens and pencils.** The test administrator probably supplies them anyway, but being prepared is always a good idea, just in case!

✔ **Prepare any food or drinks you need to take with you.**

✔ **Avoid tea, coffee, alcohol, and spicy or strong food.** These items can all disturb your sleep and make you feel tired the next day.

✔ **Take some light exercise.** Try a brisk 20-minute walk in the early evening.

✔ **Don't play a video game or watch an overly stimulating film.** You'll find it harder to 'switch off'.

✔ **Go to bed at your normal time, unless you generally stay up late, in which case try going to bed a little earlier.**

✔ **Do something that you know helps you to relax.** Some people find a bath helpful before bed, others prefer a little light reading (though not about tests!).

On the morning of the test itself:

✔ **Get up slightly earlier than usual.** You won't feel rushed.

✔ **Eat breakfast.** Don't overdo the coffee. Drink plenty of fresh fruit juice or water to re-hydrate yourself after sleep.

No matter how nervous you feel, eating beforehand is important. Your performance suffers if you have an empty stomach.

✔ **If you're awake earlier than usual, don't force yourself into eating a large breakfast.** Eating small amounts regularly is a much better way to catch up.

✔ **Leave the practice examples alone now.** Working on the examples at this stage just makes you feel nervous. Concentrate on being organised and in control.

✔ **Make sure that you have some cash on you.** Some companies still offer candidates a drink from a coffee machine or canteen and expect them to pay!

✔ **Make sure that you have the organisation's telephone contact details.**

✔ **Leave your home in plenty of time.** Turning up late without any notice is always a bad move. If you may be late, call and let the organisation know, and give an estimated time of arrival. Recruiters know candidates get delayed, and try to be accommodating. What they can't stand is candidates not arriving on time without a courtesy call.

Last-minute nerves

Experienced administrators know to positively encourage, almost to the point of ordering, candidates to visit the toilet before a test starts. Candidates announcing they need to go in the middle can cause administrative problems. Also, nervous candidates have been known to go the toilet during a test and not come back!

Arriving for the Test

You may *appear* to be the only candidate, but the recruiters know how previous applicants, and possibly current job-holders, have performed on the test. If testing is used early in the recruitment process (for instance, to carry out a first screen of candidates based on their numerical ability), a large number of candidates is likely – perhaps as many as 20 or 30 per session. The later in the process testing is used, the fewer candidates there are.

The number of candidates tested in a session also depends on the organisation's facilities. The practicalities of test administration mean that you're unlikely to be in a group larger than 6–8 people, and if the session involves more than one activity (for example, presentations or interviews), there may well be fewer.

What if I can't make it?

Recruiters are under pressure to appoint and need to adopt an overall strategy to allow them to do so. If you're the only candidate and are ill on the day, or have some other problem that may affect your performance, many organisations try to reschedule the session for you. After all, they *want* good candidates. When they have more candidates and activities, however, you're less likely to be accommodated. You can't really ask a number of candidates to come back on a different day because one candidate can't make it, and rescheduling an assessment day, with the required assessors and facilities, is a logistical challenge.

Recruiters – they're not all bad

A testing session for a job isn't like being back at school. I recall a few exchanges along the following lines:

Liam: 'Sir, the dog ate my revision notes!'

Teacher: 'Tough, get on with it.'

Recruiters do try to take extenuating circumstances into account – unlike some of *my* teachers at school (and my dog was *always* eating my revision notes, homework, school tie, you name it!).

Recruiters sometimes like to keep candidates separate and unaware of each other and may assess them consecutively. So just because you think you're the only person in the frame, don't relax and think the job's yours.

When you do arrive – on time, hopefully – the following pointers can help you to prepare yourself in those last few minutes before the test begins:

- ✔ **Eat an energy bar or some fruit 30 minutes or so before the test to give you an energy boost.**

- ✔ **Avoid drinking any more coffee.** If possible, ask for a drink of water.

- ✔ **Go to the toilet, even if you don't think you need to go.**

- ✔ **Inform the administrator (in private, if necessary) of any last-minute factors that may affect your performance on the test.** If you've forgotten your glasses, are ill, or have a personal problem, for example.

If you find that the test venue or conditions are problematic – perhaps the room is excessively crowded, noisy, hot, or dark – tactfully bring it to the administrator's attention. Even if she can't solve the problem, she should take note of the fact that you raised it as an issue.

Dealing with Internet-based Testing

If you're being tested online you have more control over the process and should find the whole thing more relaxed. The drawback is that you can't ask anyone in person for help or advice.

Here are some tips for dealing with an Internet-based test:

- ✔ **If you feel that you've had no time to prepare, ask for a little longer.** You're likely to get less warning that you're being tested this way than with a face-to-face test.

- ✔ **Make sure you have your password/user ID, and the address of the Web site where you're completing the test.**

- ✔ **If the Web site has practice tests that candidates can access, make full use of them.**

- ✔ **Make sure that you know the time window in which you have to log on.** Some passwords are time sensitive.

- ✔ **Pay attention to any technical instructions you're given regarding setting up your PC.** Some online tests require you to do things such as enabling cookies or disabling firewalls and anti-virus programs on your computer. Most online tests take you through a few procedures to make sure that everything works as it should on your computer.

- ✔ **Don't log in and out just to have a quick look at the questions.** Your password probably expires as soon as you do, and test servers keep records of everyone who logs in and when, and how long they spend on the system.

- ✔ **Read the online terms and conditions of the test carefully.** These should address the organisation's privacy policy, data protection, and your rights to feedback. If you need clarification, ask before starting the test.

- ✔ **If you can log in at home at a time of your own choosing, pick a time when you can guarantee you aren't going to be disturbed.** Avoid doing the test when you've just had a stressful day at work.

  - • **Be ruthless with your privacy.** Turn off your mobile, move the main telephone out of the room, and lock the door!

- **Don't try to squeeze in an online test between other tasks.** Get all your chores done so you can sit down to log in with a clear mind.

- **Adopt an exam mentality when you log in, even if you're on your own.** Doing so helps you stay focused.

✔ **Try to avoid doing the test at work.** You aren't at your most relaxed in a busy office, especially if your employer doesn't know that you've applied for another job!

✔ **Even if you feel that drinking relaxes you, don't sit with a glass of wine or can of beer while you're doing the test!**

Even though the test session may be unsupervised, don't let other people offer to help you, or have information to hand that you aren't allowed. Most online tests explicitly say that you must do the test alone and without any assistance at all. You may have to explicitly confirm that you understand this rule. Do exactly what the test instructions tell you. I hate to use the word, but having someone help you with an online test is *cheating*.

An online test is still just a test, all that has changed is the administration medium.

Managing Your Stress Levels

Stress is the response you have when the demands you perceive yourself as being placed under exceed your own perceived capacity to cope. A small amount of stress can be beneficial, but high levels affect your performance, and can create a vicious cycle – high levels of stress cause you to worry even more about your performance. Here are a few tips for dealing with stress:

✔ **Pay attention to what your body is telling you. Be aware of tensing your facial, shoulder, or back muscles.** Frowning or gritting your teeth are sure signs that you are too wound up.

✔ **If you're stressed, have a stretch to relieve muscle tension.** A trip to the toilet before the test session is one way of getting a few minutes to de-stress in private!

Taking care of the candidate

Although the assessment process is meant to be challenging, it shouldn't actually harm anyone. Facing up to your fears and working under pressure are important elements of many jobs, and how you deal with the test session tells recruiters a lot about you, and perhaps also tells you a lot about yourself. If I think a candidate is in real distress, I tactfully remove them from the process and look at alternative ways of carrying out the assessment.

Remember, it's only a job.

✔ Maintain an upright and relaxed posture.

✔ Take slow deep breaths, and watch out that you don't hyperventilate.

✔ Remember these key points:

- You'll probably do better on the test than you think you will.

- Tests are meant to push you, so expect to feel under pressure.

- All the other candidates are just as nervous as you – no matter what they say to the contrary!

If you really feel as though you're struggling, excuse yourself from the session; don't push yourself to the point of harm. Although excusing yourself may disqualify you from the rest of the selection process, you need to ask yourself whether the job is actually worth that amount of stress.

A poor performance is not the end of the world. Other jobs and other opportunities are always out there.

Sighing with Relief After the Test

When the test is over you may feel the urge to just relax and let your brain go into neutral. After all, it's been working hard and may need a rest! You need to keep your focus, though, because you're still under exam conditions. This is for two reasons: first, the administrator has to keep the test materials under tight control, and must collect in all material when the test is finished. Second, this period is when you find out the next steps in the process. Recruiters often have to change their schedules, usually when some candidates don't turn up for the test and the recruiter has unexpected gaps in her timetable. In this case, the recruiter may offer you the chance to wait while the test is scored and then go straight in for feedback, instead of going home and waiting for the organisation to contact you.

If you think you've done badly on a test, please don't do a midnight flit. Ability tests are designed to be hard (that's the whole point), so at least hang around for the results – they may not be as bad as all that.

All recruiters have an ethical responsibility to ensure that candidates are in at least as good a condition when they leave as they were when they arrived. Enlightened organisations encourage candidates to discuss the implications of their test results in the context of their wider career options, especially if they're unsuccessful in their application, or their test results aren't what they hoped for. Have a look at Chapter 4 for more information about receiving feedback on your test performance.

The two deadly sins of interviewing

You may think that I'm being harsh about the traditional unstructured interview, but when the recruiter and candidate engage in an unstructured, free-for-all interview we often see the *primacy* and *recency effects*.

The primacy effect is the tendency for candidates who appear earlier in the selection process to stick more in recruiters' minds.

The recency effect is the tendency for candidates who appear later in the selection process to stick more in recruiters' minds.

Primacy and recency effects can also apply to what an individual candidate says during interview, or observed group exercise, especially if the selector doesn't keep structured notes and evaluate them objectively. All this means that different candidates, and even different things a single candidate says within an interview, can be given different emphasis by a recruiter and may not always be considered in a balanced or consistent way.

One of the main benefits of psychometric testing, for both the candidate and the recruiter, is that it removes much of the opportunity for unconscious sources of bias, such as primacy and recency effects, to creep into the assessment.

Chapter 4

Dealing with Feedback

● ●

In This Chapter

▶ Obtaining your feedback

▶ Understanding why feedback is so important

▶ Knowing what to avoid

▶ Salvaging a poor test performance

▶ Considering your options

▶ Being aware of your rights

● ●

*T*est results alone often don't say much about a candidate's actual work performance. Your chance to really understand what your results mean comes in your feedback session. Here, you have the opportunity to explain to the recruiter how your test results work in real life.

Feedback is often the most overlooked element of psychometric testing. Although some candidates don't get feedback at all, most do in one form or another. In this chapter I talk about how to ensure that you do get feedback; I also suggest some questions you can ask to make sure that you understand what your results and their implications actually mean. Finally I look at how to deal with situations where your results aren't as good as you hoped.

Understanding What Feedback Can Do

Good recruiters know that simply taking the results from a test and not discussing them further with you, the candidate, is rarely enough for either party – for three main reasons:

Feedback can help to explain a low test score

To illustrate why feedback is so crucial in personality testing in particular, consider a candidate who has a low score on a personality test *self-esteem* scale (for more on personality tests, see Chapter 14). On that basis alone you may doubt whether he's up to the demands of a highly challenging job. In practice, however, I often see that candidates can use a low level of self-esteem as a very powerful motivator that can drive them on to great things. Without detailed feedback I can't say whether this applies in this case, and I may lose out on a very good candidate. Some of the most successful people I see are successful *because* they have a chip on their shoulder!

Recruiters dispense with feedback at their peril.

✔ **Applying the results to real life.** With ability tests in general, and personality profiles in particular, predicting with 100 per cent certainty how you'll behave in real life is nigh on impossible. Going through your test results to look for evidence to support (or refute) the results is vital. This process enables the recruiter to see how the results translate into performance at work.

If a recruiter sees evidence during feedback that contradicts your test results, he's wise to modify his interpretation of your characteristics and abilities. An example is when a candidate has an attack of nerves that causes a poor numerical ability test performance. If the recruiter then bases his decision on the test score alone he may be missing out on seeing the complete picture. During feedback, the candidate may be able to provide evidence from his previous work history showing that he's actually very good at numerical reasoning.

✔ **Accuracy.** Tests and the testing process contain several sources of error. One source is candidate-related errors such as misunderstanding instructions, misinterpreting questions, and nerves! Test-related sources of error can include confusing questions, poor administration or scoring procedures, and insufficient research into and clarity about what the test actually measures. A test score doesn't always reflect a candidate's true ability or character, and experienced recruiters know that a test score is often not the end of the story.

✔ **Ethics.** If you put the effort in, and provide (often very personal) information about yourself in a test, getting to know the results is only fair. In the case of an unsuccessful application, feedback can provide you with an objective and structured understanding of your development needs, future training options, and career prospects. Even if you're a successful candidate, you can still benefit from receiving ideas for further development. In my experience, candidates can find receiving no feedback at all very demoralising.

Receiving Your Feedback

You may want to discuss your options after taking a test, and take advantage of the chance to open up in a confidential setting. Even when you're not offered feedback, you are still within your rights to ask for it.

A feedback interview lasts from 15 minutes to a couple of hours or more, depending on the test results that need to be discussed, and the complexity of the job in question. The person responsible for making the selection decision generally provides the feedback, although with simple basic ability tests this job may be delegated to a more junior person. In all cases though, the person giving the feedback should be trained and qualified to do so.

Although it's the preferred method, feedback isn't always offered on a face-to-face basis. You may receive it over the telephone, by e-mail, or even by letter. Some online tests give you immediate feedback on your test results.

The downside of these less interactive methods is that asking questions and discussing your options with the recruiter may be trickier than in a face-to-face situation. If you have trouble understanding your results, try to arrange a telephone conversation with the recruiter to explore the areas you need explained.

Avoiding Common Pitfalls During Feedback

Fortunately, serious problems and pitfalls are rare. Being co-operative is the best approach. Recruiters are likely to be very experienced, and often act as an advice resource themselves – but not when you're openly hostile towards them.

Letting your emotions get the better of you and saying or doing things in the heat of the moment that you may regret later is all too easy during the stress of the feedback process. Here are a few tips to bear in mind:

✔ Stay alert even if you receive bad news – keep your brain in gear so that you can absorb the feedback.

✔ Ask questions if you don't understand something, or you miss out on feedback that may benefit you. Don't sit there in silence.

✔ Be honest and co-operate with the recruiter. If you score poorly on a numerical test, and struggle with numerical problems in real life, don't say that they present no problems for you or you may face difficulties in your job further down the line.

✔ Try not to criticise the test, the testing process, or the recruiter's competence without good reason. The recruiter may have a more in-depth awareness of the wider process than you think, and unwarranted criticism may not come across as constructive. If you don't agree with the results, be prepared to back up your argument with evidence.

✔ Avoid demanding to see information about other candidates so that you can second-guess the recruiter's decision. Information about other candidates is confidential and subject to the same legal protection as yours. The internal mechanics of the selection process may also be commercially sensitive and subject to legal privilege. You're unlikely to be aware of all the considerations in the decision-making process.

✔ Don't demand to sit the test again, or complain about an unfair element of the test or testing process that you have previously failed to bring to the recruiter's attention, unless you have a verifiable and sound reason.

Doing so can compromise the fairness of the process because it means that you have a second chance at the assessment when the other candidates don't.

✔ Don't make notes during the interview because recruiters really don't like it – they feel as though you're interviewing them! You miss key points and can't concentrate on providing additional information. Wait until the end of the session and ask if the recruiter can summarise your key strengths and weaknesses and whether you can jot down a few bullet points.

✔ Don't ask for copies of test materials, even just to help you practice – doing so doesn't get you anywhere. Test publishers forbid copying, and qualified test users have an obligation to maintain the security of test materials. Many carbonised answer sheets have the marking scale 'built-in' and show the correct answers. They simply can't be released into the public domain.

✔ Remember that an organisation doesn't have to give you careers advice. Check beforehand whether you have the opportunity to discuss your career options, and avoid harassing recruiters when such advice isn't part of the organisation's plan.

In the UK, the British Psychological Society awards the industry standard qualifications that enable a recruiter to use psychometric tests. Both A and B level qualifications exist. Anyone can go on courses to obtain these qualifications, but they can be expensive and time-consuming to complete. Most of the major test publishers don't supply test materials without evidence of these qualifications.

Everything a test user should be

Qualified, competent, and ethical test users – the people responsible for choosing which test to use and for interpreting the test results – adhere to nationally recognised training standards. You should have little to fear from their tests or from their feedback to you. Remember also that, by law, they must treat the personal information you provide as confidential, and make that information available only to people who are directly involved in the selection process.

Be aware of the difference between not *liking* the results of a test, and not *agreeing* with them. In the heat of the moment, telling the difference can be tough!

Rescuing a Poor Test Performance During Feedback

Wouldn't life be brilliant if you were always at your best and performed fantastically in tests? Unfortunately, life isn't like that! Your ability test scores may be below par, or you may have certain personality traits that aren't what the recruiter is looking for. However, all is not lost! Stay switched on during feedback because you can have a few tricks up your sleeve to help maximise your prospects. This section gives you some ideas.

Checking the results are accurate

Human error can creep into the administrative aspects of test scoring and recording, especially when large numbers of candidates are tested. If your ability test score is well below what you expected, or your personality profile sounds like that of a complete stranger, make sure that the correct results are against your name and that the scoring has been accurate.

Be careful how you ask for this information – don't back yourself into a corner by saying something like, 'That's wrong; please check it!' Say instead, 'I thought I'd done a lot better than that; that doesn't really sound like me at all. Is it possible the scores have been mixed up somehow?'

The recruiter should explain which scoring system the organisation is using and check that you understand it. Don't confuse the most common method – *percentiles* – with *percentages*. A percentage is the proportion of the questions you get right; a percentile is where your score falls in relation to the norm group. A score of 70 per cent correct may be at the 90th percentile – that is, better than the scores obtained by 90 per cent of the norm group.

To make things simple, ask for your scores in a straightforward A to E scale, where C is the average.

Understanding how your strengths can impair test results

Believe it or not, character strengths, such as being methodical and cautious, can actually slow you down during a test. Knowing how your personality may affect your performance on an ability test helps you out when your ability test scores aren't the best they could be. Although making things up is something to avoid, do consider whether any of the following personality traits (which on the face of it seem perfectly laudable) may have impacted on your strategy during an ability test:

- Cautious and careful people prefer to work at a slow, steady pace rather than rushing.
- Conscientious people make sure that they have the correct answer before moving on, and they don't like guessing.
- Detail-orientated people are very methodical, can be meticulous, and take time to double-check their answers.
- Systematic and logical people work through the questions in order, and don't skip those that they find difficult.

You can see how, in a speed-based ability test, some of the above characteristics may produce an artificially low ability score for you. If you think that you *are* the sort of person who has some of the above personality characteristics, consider whether modifying your approach to a test (for example, by trying to work faster on an ability test) may produce a more accurate result for you. Likewise, if you're a competitive and enthusiastic person who tends to rush into things, slowing yourself down may produce a better result on an ability test. You know yourself better than anyone, and thinking about how the style in which you approach an ability test can affect your performance is worthwhile.

During feedback, don't be afraid to point out factors like those above that you feel can provide the recruiter with a better, or more qualified, understanding of your results. Always be honest, though – don't claim to be a careful and methodical person when you know you're not.

Identifying factors that can affect your performance

Various issues affect the test performances of even the most focused candidates. You have control over some factors through your test preparation, and can minimise the effects of others over which you have less control.

Lack of experience is a significant factor that can adversely affect your performance. 'Practice' effects are well documented in ability test situations – the more experience you have, the better you do. That's the whole point of this book!

'Environmental' issues that can affect your performance include noise levels, lighting, comfort, interruptions, problems due to disabilities or other requirements that aren't properly dealt with at the time, and even other candidates' behaviour. Experienced test administrators know the importance of minimising environmental disturbances and distractions, and generally do their best to do so. Refer to Chapter 3 for advice on what to do if you arrive at the test venue and find that you can't sit the test in comfort. With an online test, *you* are the person with control over the environment, and thinking about how you want your immediate surroundings organised, as if you were doing the test in pencil-and-paper exam conditions, can be a good idea.

Other reasons for not doing well on an ability test can include starting too slowly, or not realising how quickly time was passing.

I recommend treading carefully if you raise any concerns. Try phrasing them as questions. For example, 'Was the test supposed to be only 25 minutes long?', rather than 'You made a right pig's ear of that test, didn't you!' Raising a concern only when faced with a set of poor results doesn't look too good.

Be careful about saying that your nerves got the better of you during the test. Doing so may cause the organisation to wonder how well you can handle pressure.

Asking for advice

If you've been unsuccessful in your test, a good idea is to end the feedback session by asking for advice such as, 'How can I improve my weaknesses?' and 'What job do you think I may be better suited to?' One question to always ask is, 'Are there any other opportunities in your organisation which you think I may be better suited to?' Enthusiasm and motivation go a long way to impress recruiters, and I have seen them change their mind about a candidate right at the last minute, simply because the candidate didn't let his head go down.

Turning Problems into Opportunities

Psychometric tests can be a real eye-opener for many people. Some candidates report that when they've been through a thorough assessment process, a lot of things begin to make sense to them. Time taken to honestly appraise yourself is always time well spent.

Applying the results to what you know about yourself

Ultimately, you have to be honest with yourself. If you score poorly on a test, or if your personality profile suggests that you're someone who doesn't have high levels of assertiveness or social confidence, take the opportunity to ask yourself some searching questions and have a rethink. You may be doing yourself a bigger favour than you realise.

For instance, if your numerical reasoning score is below average, ask yourself: 'Do I struggle with problems that are numerical in nature?' If your verbal ability scores are below average, ask: 'Do I struggle to make points in an argument?'. If your personality profile suggests that you are introverted by nature, ask: 'Do I prefer solitary hobbies or jobs where I don't have to deal with other people?'

Taking time to think things through

Many people are forced into making career decisions before they've had any real experience of the world of work. Not until they begin to apply for jobs do they discover this reality. Don't get too downhearted if you find yourself in this position. Instead, look at what you've found out about yourself as a result of the testing process, and think about what type of job your talents may be better suited to. Being forced to consider your options in the light of poor test results is an opportunity for development, not a problem.

In the end, a disappointing set of results may be one of the best things that ever happened to you.

Knowing Your Rights

Internet-based testing now means that many recruiters have access to test reports without having to be qualified to use the test that generated them – they may use a third-party Web site to do the assessment, interpretation, and report writing. Remember that the recruiter may not be in a position, or qualified, to give you feedback on your test results.

Under Data Protection legislation you can request to see any information another person or organisation holds about you. Although you do have the right to receive feedback on your test results in some form, in practice you may find this feedback difficult to obtain.

For an organisation to have a policy of refusing to give feedback is rare. If a job attracts a large number of applications, however, providing feedback only to successful candidates as a matter of course is reasonable. In this type of situation, the organisation may require unsuccessful candidates to apply for feedback.

Acquiring feedback from the recruiting organisation is always a worthwhile aim (see the earlier section 'Understanding What Feedback Can Do' for a list of the benefits). But if the organisation is not forthcoming with feedback you may prefer to chalk the whole encounter down to experience and focus on the next job, rather than invoking your rights to receive feedback under Data Protection law.

Part II
Finding Out About Different Types of Tests

'Right — you were pretty good on the speed tests — now we come to the intelligence test ....'

In this part . . .

This part is where I get you to start thinking! Trying out lots of practice tests is a great way of getting ready for the big day, but to improve your ability you need to develop your understanding of what tests are really about, and practise at a more reflective level.

In this part I use examples to show you what test questions designed to measure verbal, numerical, abstract, and technical ability look like in real life. I also explain how personality is measured, because the technique used to measure personality is very different to that used to assess ability. Consequently, the approach that you, the candidate, need to take is also very different.

In each chapter I also suggest some ways in which you can develop your skills at dealing with that particular type of test.

Chapter 5

Finding the Right Words: Verbal Ability Tests

*V*erbal ability is a strange thing. You begin to develop your verbal ability even before you're born. The process continues as you grow up, and you get better and better without even noticing. Most of us have a level of verbal ability that is perfectly suited for enabling us to live our lives in our complex society. Actually, the level of verbal ability that humans have, even from a very early age, is astonishing.

In many jobs – especially higher level ones – employers need people who can communicate effectively, both vocally and in written form. Those employers look for a level of performance that is above and beyond what you need for going about your normal day to day life.

In this chapter I describe the different elements of verbal ability, take you through a few example questions for each element, and finally look at how you can give yourself a good chance when you face a verbal ability test.

Understanding What Verbal Ability Tests Measure

Your *verbal ability* is your proficiency in the use and understanding of language and your ability to solve word-based problems. Verbal ability comprises *spelling* (how you combine letters into words), *grammar* (how you organise words to convey information), and *comprehension* (how well you understand what the words are meant to convey). You can also take higher-level verbal ability tests known as *critical thinking* tests. These tests are more commonly used when the jobholder is required to deal with large amounts of complex verbal information, such as contracts or management reports.

You can be asked to complete a number of different tasks when taking a verbal ability test. These tasks range from spotting wrong spellings and identifying correct ones to solving word-based problems such as adding a missing word to a sentence. How important these tasks are to the job you're applying for determines which tasks you have to complete. For a clerical position, for example, spelling and grammar may be most relevant. For managerial, executive, or professional-level roles, you're more likely to be given a word-based problem to solve. The problem solving tasks are usually called reasoning tests.

Dealing with spelling tests

Your brain is a smart cookie, and does a lot of work on autopilot without bothering you with the boring details. Spelling tests spoil all this lovely automatic processing and get you to do something you probably haven't done in years – build up words one letter at a time.

You'd think I could do it by now!

'Gauge' is a word I always struggle with – and I have no idea why. If I have to spell 'gauge', I normally need at least a couple of attempts to get the spelling right, and I need to build the word up a letter at a time. If you think your spelling is a bit dodgy, don't worry – everybody has pet words they struggle to spell. You're in great company!

Example of a spelling speed test question

Here is the simplest form of spelling test. This type of test tends to have around 40 to 60 questions, and you're typically allowed 20–25 minutes to complete it. This example shows you different spellings of the same word and asks you to identify the correct one.

Which of these is correct?

(a) garrolous (b) garruless (c) garroulous (d) garrulous (e) none of them

The correct answer is (d).

Examples of spelling power test questions

The other common form of spelling test asks you to pick out any incorrectly spelled words from a passage of text. You need to consider the spelling of several words, rather than just one. In addition, the question subject matter itself introduces irrelevant 'noise' into the equation to throw you off. This type of test tends to have around 30 to 50 questions, and you're typically allowed 20–25 minutes to complete it.

Which word is spelled incorrectly?

Fastidious as ever, Anthony spent what seemed like an infinite amount of time orchestrating the positions of his family until he was happy the photograph would be just right. His grandmother insisted she had the most prominant place.

(a) fastidious (b) infinite (c) orchestrating (d) prominant

The correct answer is (d).

Try this sneaky example (I've already helped you a bit):

Underline any words that are spelled incorrectly.

The politician sat forlornly at his desk reading the letter of resignation he had just written. He hoped he had gaged the mood of his constituency accurately. His conscience was not bothering him that much, cognisant as he was of how lucrative the publication of his memoirs would be.

The only incorrectly spelled word here is '*gaged*', which should of course read '*gauged*'. Don't assume that the complex words are the wrongly spelled ones. The other tricky words are only there to throw you off track.

Reading each word individually and trying not to get bogged down in the meaning of the text as a whole is the best way of dealing with this type of question. Remember as well that the *context* of the question can determine the correct spelling of a word. For example, *advise* and *advice* are both correct spellings, but in the context of 'she took her friend's advise', *advice* is the correct spelling to use.

Remember that your brain sees words in one go as whole entities. Trusting your gut instinct in a spelling test is sometimes the best way to go. The response that you *feel* is the correct answer, probably is.

Dealing with grammar tests

You learn grammar from an early age. Grammar is an important skill to acquire because it allows you to organise words in a way that enables you to be understood, and allows you to understand what other people mean.

Examples of grammar power test questions

All grammar tests can be viewed as power tests. This type of test tends to have around 30 questions, and you're typically allowed 25–30 minutes to complete it. Try these questions for size:

> **Write down the grammatically correct version of the statements below. If you think the statement *is* grammatically correct, write 'correct'.**
>
> **(a) Pass me them pencils.**
>
> _____
>
> **(b) There were less cars on the road in 1981 than there are now.**
>
> _____

The correct answers are (a) Pass me *those* pencils; (b) There were *fewer* cars on the road in 1981 than there are now. See the 'Improving Your Verbal Ability' section later in this chapter for ideas on how to brush up your grammar.

Remember to relax. You often don't know the correct answer with 100 per cent certainty in verbal ability tests. Just use your best judgement and move on to the next question.

Dealing with comprehension tests

Comprehension is to do with understanding information, and is tied up with spelling and grammar (in the sense that you need a decent level of both to be able to take in information at all). The comprehension bit comes in when you have to start making sense of that information.

Examples of comprehension speed test questions

This type of test generally asks you questions to test how well you understand some given information. These tests tend to contain around 40 to 60 questions and you're typically allowed 30–40 minutes to complete them.

Comprehension speed tests can take several different forms, but they all tend to follow the same theme. I've presented four types here separately, but you may find elements of each presented in a single test.

This type of test looks at words that are related to each other:

> **Which word can be attached to both of these to make two new expressions?**
>
> **Still — Sentence**
>
> (a) frame (b) live (c) life (d) word (e) none of these

The correct answer is (c).

This next type of test asks you to fill in missing words:

> **Complete this sentence using one of the words that follow, so that it makes sense:**
>
> **Exercise is _____ for you – doctors recommended we need at least 20 minutes of cardiovascular exercise a day.**
>
> (a) exercise (b) supposed (c) good (d) fast
> (e) none of these

The correct answer is (c).

This next question looks at *synonyms* (words with the same meaning):

Which word means the same as saturated?

(a) drench (b) drenched (c) douse (d) drying
(e) none of these

The correct answer is (b).

This next type of question looks at *antonyms* (opposite words) and can be quite tricky:

What is the opposite of notable?

(a) unremarkable (b) venerable (c) noticeable
(d) un-notable (e) none of these

The correct answer is (a).

When choosing opposites, watch out for words that don't exist, but are made up by simply putting *un* or *dis*, or something similar, at the start of a word.

Examples of comprehension power test questions

Candidates often report that comprehension power tests are the hardest type of test they come across, and you can see why. Unlike numerical tests where you can work out the correct answer with 100 per cent certainty, verbal tests rely on what you *judge* the correct answer to be. Usually you have to decide whether a statement is true or not based on information you're given. You have to ignore what you already know. If the question tells you that the moon is made of cheese, that's what you need to believe.

Read the following and then answer the questions beneath. Base your answers only on what you read:

Alan and David had a discussion about how many times they had been stung in their lives. Alan said he had only ever been stung twice, both times by bees. David thought he had been stung by a bee, and a few times by ants. Alan told David he wasn't sure whether ants could sting. Ants can bite and some can spray formic acid. Neither of them had ever been stung by a wasp.

1. Wasps sting people.

(a) true (b) untrue (c) not enough information to say

2. David thought he had been stung by a bee.

(a) true (b) untrue (c) not enough information to say

3. Some ants can spray formic acid.

(a) true (b) untrue (c) not enough information to say

4. David thought he had been stung by a wasp when he was young.

(a) true (b) untrue (c) not enough information to say

The answers: **1.** (c) Although you may know that 'wasps sting people' to be true, the information in the text doesn't say so, or allow you to definitely imply that the statement is true (subtle, eh?); **2.** (a) This statement is true – the text says so; **3.** (a) This statement is also true – the text says so; **4.** (b) This statement is untrue – the text says so.

Verbal reasoning tests in particular can be among the most difficult of psychometric tests, simply because they ask you to slow down and do consciously what you normally do automatically – something you're not used to doing.

Improving Your Verbal Ability

Verbal skills are built up over time. Gradually improving the volume and quality of your reading improves your verbal abilities, but don't expect dramatic improvements overnight. Stick at it, and you will get better!

Here are a few more suggestions to help you improve upon the skills you already have.

✔ **Improving your spelling**

- Write down any words you come across that you find difficult to spell. Try starting with the last letter and then working to your left so that your brain has to work a bit harder!

- Use exaggerated pronunciation silently in your head when trying to remember words that you have difficulty with (for example, P-S-Y-CH-O-metric).

✔ **Improving your grammar**

- Read the broadsheet newspapers. Your brain assimilates the grammatical rules you see without too much effort on your part.

- Search the Internet for 'rules of good grammar'. Write down the key points of what you find. If you can find examples of the same sentence written using both good and poor grammar, write them down and try to create your own similar examples.

- If u txt a lot on yr mb fne thn look to c if u can c the grmr mstkes u make. (Try composing your texts longhand for a week!)

- Check out the BBC's excellent Skillswise Web site at www.bbc.co.uk/skillswise.

- Take a look at Lesley J. Ward and Geraldine Woods' excellent *English Grammar For Dummies* (Wiley).

✔ **Improving your comprehension**

- The key thing here is to develop your skills at understanding and drawing conclusions from complex information. Find a high quality newspaper, and read some of the more complex articles (the more boring the better – you won't be distracted by the actual content!). Political supplements in the Sunday papers are a good starting point. Rewrite the article using just bullet points for the key facts, and then see what information you think necessarily follows from what you've written, but which doesn't appear in the original article. Ask someone else to check your conclusions.

- Rewrite the article using fewer, or completely different, words so that the article means the same, and then the opposite.

Above all, keep practising. Improving your verbal abilities is hard at first, but gets easier as you go along!

Reading a good quality newspaper may be handy when you prepare for an interview. In response to an interviewer's question – for example 'What was the last thing you read?' – which do you think sounds better: 'The TV guide' or 'An article on the political problems of integrating new EU members'?

Chapter 6

Doing Your Sums: Numerical Ability Tests

● ●

In This Chapter

▶ Understanding what numerical ability is

▶ Comprehending the different tests used to measure numerical ability

▶ Maximising your chances on a numerical ability test

● ●

*M*any people are frightened by the prospect of doing a numerical ability test. However, you have less to worry about than you think. Numerical tests are actually among the easiest to deal with, and mathematical questions always have a definite correct answer. Mathematical rules are well established and well known, and are taught at school (although you may have forgotten some of them!). This area of testing is one in which practising improves your skills quite dramatically.

Most higher-level jobs, such as those in the areas of finance and manufacturing, require an understanding of numbers and an awareness of the information that can be obtained from numbers, tables, and figures. As a successful applicant, you may even need to do some number crunching yourself. Many managers have to cope with numerical information such as financial reports, sales figures, and staff salaries as an incidental part of their job, so expect to face a numerical test for most managerial positions.

In this chapter I describe the different elements of numerical ability, take you through some example questions for each element, and look at how you can give yourself the best chance when facing a numerical ability test.

Understanding What Numerical Ability Tests Measure

Numerical ability tests measure two things:

- ✓ **Your ability to carry out basic numerical calculations such as addition and multiplication.** Calculations use basic mathematical rules and if you don't use those rules regularly you can easily forget them!

- ✓ **Your ability to apply your numerical calculation skills to solving real-life problems.** Tests that ask you to make sense of information before doing calculations are often referred to as numerical *reasoning*, rather than numerical *ability* tests.

Dealing with basic mathematical ability tests

Basic numerical ability tests ask you to perform calculations with context-free data. They usually present you with a partial calculation to complete.

Examples of numerical ability speed tests

Here are some examples that involve calculations only of a single type (for example, addition). Tests like this are common. They tend to last between 25 and 30 minutes and may contain between 40 and 60 questions.

In the following questions you need to choose what you think the question mark represents from the list of possible answers provided. If you have to work out what a letter represents, don't have an algebra panic! Just imagine the word '[blank]' instead of the letter.

1. 2 + 7 + 9 + 34 = ?

  (a) 50   (b) 52   (c) 53   (d) 58   (e) none of these

2. 139 – 23 – 5 = ?

  (a) 101   (b) 108   (c) 111   (d) 148   (e) none of these

3. $2 \times 5 \times 8 = ?$

(a) 0   (b) 80   (c) 82   (d) 88   (e) none of these

4. $58 \div 2 = ?$

(a) 18   (b) 23   (c) 27   (d) 29   (e) none of these

The correct answers are: **1.** (b); **2.** (c); **3.** (b); **4.** (d).

These types of question aren't usually too difficult. As with all speed tests, working quickly is the key. If you get stuck on a question, leave it and move on to the next.

Examples of numerical ability power tests

Power tests require more thought. They often combine different mathematical calculations and *nested* calculations (calculations in brackets that you need to work out before you can proceed with the rest of the question). Tests like this are common. They tend to last between 30 and 40 minutes and may contain between 30 and 40 questions. Try these illustrative examples:

1. $(2 + 3) \times 8 = ?$

(a) 16   (b) 24   (c) 32   (d) 40   (e) none of these

2. $(^{10}\!/_{20})/2 = ?$

(a) 0   (b) 1   (c) 1/2   (d) 2   (e) none of these

3. $(1 + z)/2 = 1$

What is z ?

(a) 3   (b) –3   (c) –2   (d) 1   (e) none of these

4. $25 \times t = 500$

What is t ?

(a) 20   (b) 10   (c) 25   (d) 50   (e) none of these

5. $^{3}\!/_{5} = ?$

(a) 0.2   (b) 0.3   (c) 0.6   (d) 0.15   (e) none of these

6. $150 \times 800 = ?$

(a) 120000   (b) 12001   (c) 1600   (d) 8500
(e) none of these

7. $5 \times (-4) = ?$

(a) 0   (b) 10   (c) –20   (d) 20   (e) none of these

The correct answers are: **1.** (d); **2.** (e); **3.** (d); **4.** (a); **5.** (c); **6.** (a); **7.** (c).

These questions show how you can get to the right answer by applying reasoning instead of just pure maths. For example, in Question 6, you can work out the answer by counting the zeros in the question. Because these zeros are being multiplied, the answer must end in at least three zeros. This then enables you to narrow your options to **6a** or **6e**, and then calculating $15 \times 8 = 120$ gets you quickly to the answer **6a**.

If a numerical ability speed test contains different types of calculations, you may find it easier to quickly skim over the ones you know you find hard and do the ones you find easier first. Many people find division and multiplication questions hard to answer, so concentrate on doing the addition and subtraction questions first.

Dealing with numerical reasoning tests

Now the tests start to get a bit more complicated, with questions that ask you to apply your numerical skills to solving problems. These examples present you with information that you need to digest and understand before you can go any further. You may also need to do some calculations that the question doesn't ask you for, just to get you to that point. The calculations you finally perform to answer the actual questions are often quite simple. The hard part is working out what those calculations need to be!

In numerical reasoning tests you're left to decide which calculations you need to perform in order to arrive at the correct answer. The emphasis is on your understanding of the information, rather than on your ability to do calculations.

Examples of numerical reasoning speed tests

Speed tests are the slightly easier form of numerical *reasoning* test. They ask you to make sense of information, but don't give you too much in one go. Crucially, numerical reasoning speed tests leave you to decide what calculations you need to perform in order to answer the question.

Numerical reasoning speed tests have around 30 or more questions and last up to 45 minutes.

Understanding what is described to you before you answer the questions is key here. Here are some examples:

Fill in the missing data (?):

1	2	4
2	4	8
4	8	?

The correct answer is 16, because that number satisfies the pattern upon which the grid is based: the numbers double as you move across the grid horizontally, they also double as you move down the grid vertically, and they multiply by 4 as you move diagonally from the top-left corner.

Another popular question format asks you to identify a rule linking a sequence of numbers, and then apply the rule to determine the next number in the sequence.

Which number comes next?

1   4   9   16

(a) 20   (b) 25   (c) 27   (d) 35

The correct answer is (b). The sequence is produced by squaring 1, 2, 3, 4, and 5 in turn.

A variation on this theme presents you with the data as shown below and asks you to work out the missing value. (This example uses the same rule as the example above):

Which number should replace the question mark?

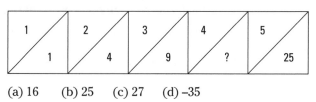

(a) 16   (b) 25   (c) 27   (d) –35

The correct answer is (a). The same rule is at work here as in the preceding example.

Examples of numerical reasoning power tests

Numerical reasoning power tests are more complex. You're presented with information that can be very detailed, and which commonly relates to a business issue. Tests like this tend to last from 45 to 60 minutes and may only contain 10 to 12 sets of data, each with 5 to 10 questions.

As with numerical reasoning speed tests, the key is to read and understand the information you're presented with before trying to answer the questions. Here are some examples:

The table below shows the amount of torque produced by three different engines at three different rpm (revolutions per minute).

Engine	Torque (ft/lbs) @ 2000 rpm	Torque (ft/lbs) @ 4000 rpm	Torque (ft/lbs) @ 6000 rpm
A	100	130	150
B	120	130	220
C	115	160	210

1. Which engine produces the highest amount of torque on average across all rpm ranges? (circle the correct answer)

A   B   C

2. Which engine produces the highest torque at 6000 rpm ? (circle the correct answer)

A   B   C

3. How much more torque does engine A produce at 6000 rpm than engine C at 2000 rpm?

(a) 35   (b) 105   (c) 125   (d) 140

The correct answers are: **1.** C; **2.** B; **3.** (a).

You should note a couple of interesting things about this set of questions:

✔ The content seems complex. Not many people understand subjects such as engine torque. In fact, the content is irrelevant, and you don't need to be able to understand torque to answer the questions. The same figures and approach may also apply when you're presented with business data. You shouldn't need any specialist knowledge to deal with the actual information.

✔ The actual maths needed here is very simple. For instance, for Question 3 you only need to calculate 150 – 115 = 35. But you probably took a minute or so to work out what you needed to do.

Many numerical reasoning power tests share these two characteristics.

Numerical reasoning tests often try to blind you with science. Focus on the numbers, more than the text content, in numerical reasoning power tests and work through the data one piece at a time so you understand what you're asked to work with. Trying to take in everything at once in questions like these is overwhelming.

Improving Your Numerical Ability

For a full-scale numerical ability test, you need to be up to speed on these essential mathematical principles:

✔ Addition

✔ Subtraction

✔ Division (long and short)

✔ Multiplication (long and short)

✔ Fractions, decimals, and percentages (they're the same thing)

✔ Negative numbers

 ✔ Estimating (*very* useful)

 ✔ Ratios and proportions

 ✔ Algebra

 ✔ Averages

 ✔ Probability

Fortunately, numerical ability is one thing you can improve quite dramatically with practice. Working on your basic skills also improves your higher-level reasoning ability. Unlike grammar and spelling, where a correct example is often self-explanatory, simple exposure to numerical material doesn't help you a great deal when you don't have a grasp of the underlying mathematical rules and principles at work. Brushing up on these aspects first is important. Here are a few general tips to help get you started:

 ✔ Search the Internet for 'basic mathematical rules'. When you've identified these rules, make your own summary notes, and keep practising.

 ✔ Visit the BBC's excellent Skillswise Web site at www.bbc.co.uk/skillswise.

 ✔ Check out Mark Zegarelli's book *Basic Math and Pre-Algebra For Dummies* (Wiley).

 ✔ Write your own test questions.

Do make sure that you're fully up to speed with basic mathematical principles. When you deal with higher-level tests you draw your options from that core body of knowledge. If you don't know how to turn a fraction into a decimal (hint: use *division*), you can't bring that method into play as an option when dealing with numerical power tests.

Chapter 7

Getting all Creative: Abstract Ability Tests

. . . .

In This Chapter

▶ Understanding what abstract ability is

▶ Considering the different tests used to measure abstract ability

▶ Maximising your chances on an abstract ability test

. . . .

*A*bstract ability tests are the great levellers among psychometric tests. Tests of creativity in particular bring everyone down to the same starting point because they don't directly assess verbal or numerical skills, which are often dependent upon the level of education a person has received. People from all educational backgrounds tend to find these types of test equally difficult (or easy!).

In their more complex form abstract tests can also be used to assess strategic thinking. Organisations use these tests because they provide a good measure of how well a person can problem-solve when she has little previous experience to go on.

In this chapter I describe the different aspects of abstract ability and offer a few example questions to get you going. I also give you some tips to help you confidently approach an abstract ability test.

Understanding What Abstract Ability Tests Measure

Abstract ability involves two kinds of thought:

✔ **Creative thinking.** I don't mean creativity in the way you may be used to thinking about it. Recruiters aren't interested in your ability to draw pictures or write poetry. What they are interested in is your ability to identify solutions to novel problems – your ability to see, and then to go beyond, what is obvious.

You can view creativity as comprising a period of preparation (where you take in the nature of the problem), incubation (where you may occasionally return to thinking about the problem, but mostly let your unconscious get to work on it), illumination (where the answer suddenly comes to you 'in a flash'), and verification (where you check that what you've come up with is correct). Incubation is the key to creativity.

✔ **Strategic thinking ability.** Your ability to think strategically is about how well you can spot underlying issues and trends, make decisions and judgements, and plan strategies and solutions to achieve your objectives.

Dealing with creativity tests

Creativity tests usually present you with a set of abstract information (usually shapes or patterns) and ask you to establish a common rule or theme that links them.

Example of a creativity speed test

This example of a creativity speed test asks you to identify the theme that links a set of patterns, and then to choose the next pattern in the sequence. Creativity speed tests often take this form and may typically ask you to answer between 25 and 30 questions within a 25-minute period.

Which shape comes next in this sequence?

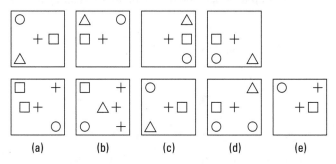

(a)   (b)   (c)   (d)   (e)

The correct answer is (c). The circle moves clockwise around the figure, the cross always remains in the centre, and the small square alternates position from left to right.

You may come across abstract tests in different formats, but they all ask you to do the same thing – make sense of confusing information. The ability being assessed doesn't change, only how the test asks you to apply that ability.

Examples of creativity power tests

Creativity power tests are more difficult because the placement of the shapes is random. Because the placement isn't sequential, you can't start by looking at one end for a systematically developing pattern to help work the answer out. This type of test tends to have 30–40 questions, and you're normally allowed 30–40 minutes to complete it.

Here, you have to think creatively to find the odd one out.

Which shape is the odd one out?

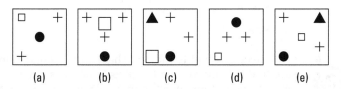

(a)   (b)   (c)   (d)   (e)

The correct answer is (b). This is the only figure with three small crosses. The others all have two.

Another form of this type of test asks you to work out the relationship between one pair of figures and apply it to another pair.

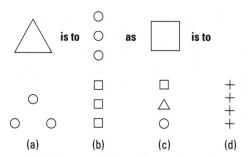

The correct answer is (d). The number of elements in the second set of the pair is the same as the number of sides contained in the first figure.

 A good tip for creativity tests is to just look at the question first without working too hard at trying to solve it. Sometimes the correct answer does just 'pop-out'.

The rules at work in creativity tests tend to be few in number, although they can occur in complex combinations. When trying to identify the rule(s) linking a series of patterns, consider the following elements:

- ✔ Colour
- ✔ Number of elements
- ✔ Orientation
- ✔ Position in the pattern
- ✔ Position in the sequence
- ✔ Shape
- ✔ Size

 If you need to identify the odd shape out in a question, make sure that the rule you find applies to all the shapes concerned, and not just most of them. If your rule doesn't explain everything you see in the question, the rule isn't correct.

 You actually improve as you work through a creativity test. When you solve a problem, the rule you discover becomes available for you to use with subsequent questions. So relax – you get better as you go on.

Dealing with strategic thinking tests

When you think strategically, you apply your creative ability to real-life situations. Many strategic thinking tests (or strategic reasoning ability tests as they are often known) don't look like they belong in a chapter about abstract thinking. They *do* look like *critical thinking* or *numerical reasoning* tests, but what they measure is fundamentally different. Strategic thinking tests measure your ability to see underlying trends and issues in a problem and, taking those into account, choose a solution that allows you to meet an objective. Not everyone agrees, but because strategic thinking tests tend to rely on more complex types of question and require a bit more thought to answer, I find considering them to be more power than speed tests most convenient.

The other unusual feature of strategic thinking tests is that very often they have no norms, and so you don't get a 'score' in the way you can with, say, a numerical ability test. So they aren't *psychometric tests* in the sense that I've been discussing them so far. However, you may well come across them in a recruitment situation, which is why I've included them here.

Because these questions often have no single correct answer and are therefore difficult to score, the recruiter may explore your responses with you in detail afterwards, perhaps combined with a formal presentation. This approach enables the recruiter to explore your judgement and decision-making processes.

Examples of strategic thinking tests

When faced with a strategic thinking test, taking an overview of the problem you're presented with is the key. Don't get bogged down in the detail. Identify what the objective is, and use that to guide you. For every solution you generate, ask *how* that solution helps you meet your objective before you commit to it. Sometimes your objective is given to you, sometimes not. You're often left to decide for yourself what your objectives should be. The format of this type of test varies widely, but typically it may present you with a single or small number of scenarios and ask you a number of questions about each. Often, these tests have no time limit. Any time limits that are applied tend to be on the longer side – perhaps an hour or more.

Strategic thinking tests are quite similar to *work sample tests*, where a problem you may face in the job you've applied for is given to you to solve.

Try this example, which presents you with your objective, and a set of options to choose from:

The Lost Walkers

You're leading a group of eight walkers across a deserted moor. Each member of your party has a backpack containing food, drink, and waterproof clothing. Your job is to ensure the safety of all the walkers.

You've timed your walk to allow for unexpected events and you have a map and know your location exactly. The time is 4 p.m. and the sun is due to set at 6 p.m. The moor becomes a very dangerous place after dark and the chances are you'd get lost once the sun goes down.

One member of your party has twisted her ankle and can't maintain the same walking speed as the others. Your map shows a shelter, and at normal walking speed you think you all may take about two hours to reach it. Unfortunately, to reach the safety of the shelter you need to leave the track and cross rough moorland.

Your other option is to press on to the end of the walk, where your minibus to transport you off the moor is waiting. What do you do?

(a) Ask the walkers to make for the shelter.

(b) Ask the walkers to leave their backpacks and head for the shelter.

(c) Ask the walkers to continue to the end of the walk as planned.

(d) Ask half the party to head for the shelter taking the injured walker with them, and half to continue to the end of the walk as planned.

The correct answer is (c). Your objective was to ensure the safety of all the walkers, and you had allowed time for unforeseen events such as injuries when you planned the hike. Option (a) would mean leading your team off the track without being able to guarantee arriving at the shelter before dark. Option (b) may speed the group up a little, but would leave them without essential supplies, and you still couldn't guarantee reaching the shelter before dark. Option (d) means splitting the group up, and half of them wouldn't be under your care. The half heading for the shelter couldn't guarantee arriving before dark.

Now try this example, which, rather than giving you a list of options from which to choose, asks you to work out what you would do.

You're In Charge

You arrive at work in the Customer Service Department of a large stationery supplier and find that two of your colleagues have called in sick. Today was always going to be busy, but now you are standing in for your boss as well. Sitting down at her desk you find in her in-tray the following items that need to be dealt with:

A returned, three-month-old unpaid invoice for ₤98.22 marked 'address not known'.

A complaint from a customer about a late delivery.

A letter from another of your customers about persistent late deliveries.

A request for an interview from a local radio station about office paper recycling.

A letter waiting to be sent to a candidate telling her that she was unsuccessful in a job application.

Minutes from a management team meeting marked 'immediate action needed', in your boss's handwriting.

A note asking you to call your business bankers.

Two customer invoices marked 'ready to post'.

How would you deal with these items?

The answer? Well, no right answer exists here. However, a recruiter wants to see you set yourself an objective. For example, to keep all existing customers happy, or to make sure that income is maximised. She also wants to see that you planned both the sequence in which you would deal with the items in the in-tray, and the actions you would take for each individual item, to help you meet those objectives.

When making decisions in strategic thinking tests, try to adopt a structured approach:

1. **Explore the nature of the problem.**

2. **Set your objective.**

3. **Identify and locate any other information you need.**

4. **Generate a few different solutions.**

5. **Test each solution in turn against your objective.**

6. **Choose the most efficient solution that lets you meet your objective.**

7. **Apply your chosen solution.**

8. **Evaluate how well the solution helped you meet your objective**

Improving Your Abstract Ability

A whole industry has grown up around helping people develop their creative and strategic thinking skills. The Internet is a good source of advice and exercises to develop your strategic thinking skills in particular. If you're serious about developing your creative and strategic thinking skills, you can find numerous training providers, each with their own take on the matter, by searching for 'improving your strategic/creative thinking'.

Creativity is difficult to develop, as much of it seems to happen unconsciously and some people just seem to be more naturally creative than others. However, you can take several steps to improve your creativity test performance:

✔ **Practise completing tests.** Practising develops your abstract ability. Working out correct solutions helps to train your mind into a more flexible thinking pattern. So, don't stop thinking about a question once you have come to the correct answer. See if you can use the examples I provide to produce a different solution yourself.

✔ **Write your own test questions.** Write your own examples from scratch, systematically applying the features I describe in the 'Examples of creativity power tests' section earlier in this chapter – colour (although colour tends not to be used that often), number of elements, orientation, position in the pattern, position in the sequence, shape, and size.

✔ **Use the examples in this book flexibly.** Keep looking for other rules that perhaps link only two or three of the shapes, even after you think you've arrived at the correct solution. To help you (and you may not think doing so is very fair!) I've provided only the correct answers to the abstract questions, and not an explanation as to *why* they are the correct answers. Figuring that out for yourself is a great way of developing your skills.

Chapter 8

Saying It Without Words: Technical Ability Tests

*T*echnical ability tests look at how well you can understand the physical aspects of how the world works. You can develop this ability, but some people naturally have better technical ability than others and can pick up rules of how the world works simply by seeing what goes on around them.

Technical ability tests are most commonly used to assess applicants for design, production, and manufacturing jobs, and for junior postings such as engineering apprenticeships and production line posts. At a basic level, employers may be satisfied that you have the required knowledge and ability when you have a technical qualification, such as a diploma or a degree in engineering. If you do, you may be less likely to face a technical ability test. For example, I wouldn't use a mechanical ability test to select an engineering manager because the best evidence of his competence in this area comes from his work history. However, without any work experience to back it up, employers may not take your qualification as a guarantee that you have the underlying ability. That's where these tests come in.

In this chapter I describe the different elements that make up your technical ability and offer you some example questions relating to those elements. To help set you off on the right foot, I also give you some tips on how to prepare yourself for a technical ability test.

Understanding What Technical Ability Tests Measure

Generally speaking, technical ability tests measure your ability to deal with and carry out practical tasks on problems that you come across in the physical world. Specifically, technical ability tests are used to measure three things:

- ✓ *Mechanical ability* – your understanding of how objects behave in the real world.

- ✓ *Spatial ability* – how well you can visualise a two-dimensional pattern made up into a three-dimensional object or changed through being manipulated in some way.

- ✓ *Detail and accuracy* – how accurately you work with detailed information.

Dealing with mechanical ability tests

Mechanical ability tests present you with a number of questions about the mechanical and physical properties of objects. They can contain questions to do with speed, heat, light, gravity, mass, weight, volume, area, and the movement of fluids and gasses. Mechanical ability tests often contain both simple and complex items, and so speed and power distinctions don't really apply.

Examples of mechanical ability tests

Mechanical ability tests tend to last from 25 to 30 minutes and may contain 20 to 30 questions. Here are a few examples:

1. A ball is released from a height of 10 centimetres. The ball loses half of its return height after every bounce. Below 1 centimetre the ball stops bouncing. How many times in total does the ball hit the ground before it comes to a halt?

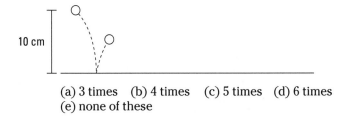

(a) 3 times   (b) 4 times   (c) 5 times   (d) 6 times
(e) none of these

The correct answer is (b). If the ball loses half of its previous height after every bounce, then after four bounces the ball would bounce less than 1 centimetre.

2. Three spacecraft, each with a different mass, are orbiting the earth at the same altitude. Which is the heaviest?

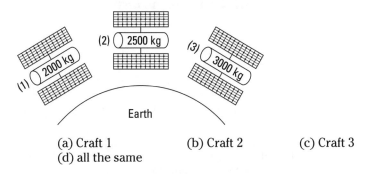

(a) Craft 1   (b) Craft 2   (c) Craft 3
(d) all the same

The correct answer is (d). Even though objects may have different masses, in the absence of gravity they weigh nothing!

3. Three cubes made of the same material are heated to the same temperature. Which cools the quickest?

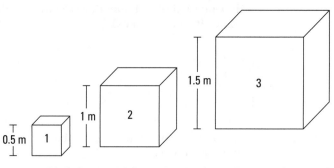

(a) Cube 1   (b) Cube 2   (c) Cube 3   (d) all the same

The correct answer is (a). Cube 1, being the smallest of the three cubes, has the largest surface-area-to-volume ratio, which helps it to lose heat the fastest.

4. Three identical balls are simultaneously rolled down three different ramps of equal height. Which ball hits the ground first?

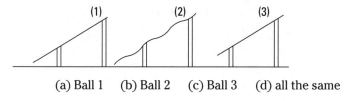

(a) Ball 1   (b) Ball 2   (c) Ball 3   (d) all the same

The correct answer is (c). Ramp 3 has the shortest length for the ball to travel before it falls directly to the ground. The fastest route is straight down.

Questions such as these tend to rely on a bit of basic knowledge (not much more than the simple science stuff you did at school), as well as a natural understanding of how the world works.

Dealing with spatial ability tests

Spatial ability tests look at your ability to mentally visualise, rotate, and manipulate objects. These tests are hard work and require a lot of concentration!

Example of a spatial ability speed test question

Spatial ability speed tests typically ask you to examine a two-dimensional figure (in other words, a figure that shows only two dimensions – usually length and width) and identify the identical object from a series of very similar objects. These tasks sound simple enough, but the figures from which you have to choose your answer are all rotated to some extent. This type of test may have around 30 questions, and you're normally allowed 20–25 minutes to complete it.

Here is an example:

Look at the first object, and then choose from those that follow the object you think is the same.

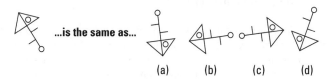

(a)　　(b)　　(c)　　(d)

The correct answer is (b).

In spatial rotation tests, try spinning your test booklet to get a different view of the figures (but I don't recommend doing so if the test is computer based!).

When you rotate an object, focus on one specific aspect of it, and eliminate potential answers based only on that aspect. Then move onto another specific aspect, and do the same until you have eliminated all the incorrect answers.

Examples of spatial ability power tests

Spatial ability power tests include more complex object rotation tasks, and ask you to construct three-dimensional objects from two-dimensional shapes. Spatial ability power tests typically contain 30–40 items and take more effort to complete, so you often have slightly longer to complete them – perhaps up to 40 minutes. Try these two examples.

Look at the first object, and then choose from those that follow the object you think is the same.

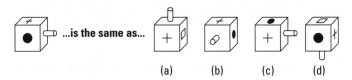

(a) (b) (c) (d)

The correct answer is (d).

Look at the unfolded shape, and then choose from those that follow the object that best represents the first shape if it were folded.

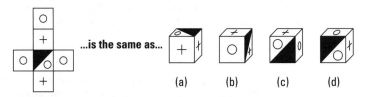

(a) (b) (c) (d)

The correct answer is (c).

 When you rotate three-dimensional objects, try to identify two sides that you know are joined and study how the characteristics of those two sides relate to each other. Working out this relationship helps to eliminate some of the incorrect choices.

Dealing with detail and accuracy tests

Many people are capable of working to a very high level of accuracy given enough time. However, jobs that require a high level of accuracy often need you to perform the work quickly and under pressure. As a result, these tests don't just assess accuracy – they also look at how fast you can work while remaining accurate.

 These tests are some of the fastest psychometric tests. They give you the least amount of time to complete the greatest number of questions.

Examples of detail and accuracy speed tests

I'm not going to mince my words here – detail and accuracy speed tests are hard work! These tests present you with information that has no real meaning. They sometimes ask you just to copy the information from one column to another. But as marking that kind of test is hard work for test scorers (they need to visually verify that what you copied was correct), you're normally asked instead to check that two given sets of information are identical. However, the method by which you have to make your responses can vary.

Detail and accuracy tests rely on your short-term memory, which can usually retain between five and nine pieces of information (which is why you can remember your home phone number more easily than your mobile number). The test items present you with more information than you can comfortably hold in your short-term memory.

Tests like these may only last a couple of minutes and can contain anything up to 40 questions. Have a look at these examples:

1. Underline any errors in the second column:

6jls8sqqvl	**6jls i8spqvl**
44487555yn	**44847555yn**

2. Which is the correct copy?

73884575447

(a) 7384575547　　(b) 7388477547　　(c) 738447547
(d) none of them

The correct answer is (d).

Examples of detail and accuracy power tests

Detail and accuracy power tests still rely on speed, but crucially the information you're given to check or copy has relevance to real life, such as data entry information. That relevance introduces a significant element of distraction into the task. So, with tests like these, you really need to ignore the subject matter and focus on the facts presented to you. Again, the time allowed for these tests can be short, perhaps only 10–15 minutes, and they may contain around 30 items.

Have a go at these two examples:

1. Underline any errors in the second column.

Mrs E. M. Watham	Mrs E. M. Watham
56 Cherry Tree Ave.	56 Cherry tree Ave.
Godalming	Gdalming
Surrey	Surrey
Tel: 7777867	Tel: 7777867
Customer Ref: WAS444653	Customer Ref: WAS444653

2. Underline any errors you find in the second table.

To: Mr C. Appleby c/o Production Manager

Invoice 344857

Repair services 4 hours @ £60 per hour	£240.00
Materials	£120.00
Travelling	£100.00
Sub-total	£460.00
VAT @ 17.5%	£262.86
Invoice total	£722.86

To: Mr C. Appelby c/o Production Manager

Invoice 344857

Repair services 4 hours at £60 per hour	£240.00
Materials	£120.00
Travelling	£100.00
Sub-total	£460.00
VAT @ 17.5%	£262.86
Invoice total	£722.86

Note that this question doesn't ask you to check that the numbers add up correctly, only that the information has been copied correctly. Don't approach this test by verifying that the actual calculations in questions are correct – that would cost you valuable time.

Your brain is good at recognising patterns. If the format of the test allows it, try to visually skip back and forth between the information sets to see if any errors jump off the page. If this strategy doesn't work for you, go back to scrutinising the detail with a fine-tooth comb.

Improving Your Technical Ability

People who are good at mechanical ability seem to have that ability because they spend their time dealing with mechanical-type problems. For instance, I understand how electricity works, but only because I once spent many months trying to diagnose the electrical problems on my old car, and then a few weeks replacing the wiring and trying to get it running. Likewise, if you studied physics at school, you're probably in a better position to answer technical ability questions than someone who didn't.

A good way to develop your spatial rotation ability (and I know this sounds odd) is by taking empty packaging boxes, unfolding them, and drawing patterns and shapes on the reverse. Finally, try to predict in your head what they'll look like when you reassemble them, and see if you're right.

Before you unfold the box you can try predicting what it will look like when unfolded.

Detail and accuracy tests rely on concentration and attention to detail. Try these tips; you may just see how little attention we pay to the small details in our everyday lives:

- ✔ Practise holding four or five bits of data in your head at a time, and see how long you can hold them before your concentration fails.
- ✔ Practise reading text backwards and then writing it down.

✔ Practise paying close attention to fine detail. When reading something, don't just skim through on autopilot – really look into what the text is saying to you.

✔ Practise focusing on an object in your environment and really scrutinising it. Write down every tiny detail you can about the object. You may be surprised at just how much detail you've never noticed before. This exercise shows just how much you can miss.

Chapter 9

Seeing the Real You: Personality Tests

*Y*our personality has an impact on all jobs you perform, so personality tests are the type of psychometric test you're most likely to come across.

In this chapter I describe how personality is characterised, look at a few practical issues to do with measuring personality, and give you a few example questions. I don't offer you any tips on how to 'maximise your chances', but talk instead about how best to approach personality tests. I do this for a very good reason – the purpose of a personality test is to produce an accurate description of your character, and the best chance you have of achieving that is to be honest in your approach.

Understanding What Personality Tests Measure

Although the whole idea of personality sounds a bit mysterious (I talk about different theories of personality in Chapter 1), a personality test is one form of assessment that you don't need to worry about.

The key feature of ability tests is that they rely on effort. Ability test questions are designed to be difficult to answer, and the more work you put into an ability test, the better you perform.

In Chapters 5–8, I classify most ability tests as *speed* or *power* tests. You can't think of personality tests in the same way because the questions are of a *zero* difficulty level – that is, the answers require no effort on your part to produce. When you've read the question, all you need to do is to indicate a preference.

So, whereas ability tests measure *maximum* performance, personality tests measure *typical* performance. For this reason, setting any kind of pass mark is pointless, as is viewing one personality profile as being 'better' than another in any general sense.

A typical personality test question may be:

I enjoy spending time on my own.

(a) agree   *(b) disagree*

The idea of having to put effort into answering a question like this makes no sense.

Personality tests help recruiters to tell how well suited your personality is to the job in question. The answer may be 'not very well', and finding this out before you turn up for work on your first day is better for you and the organisation! You can always find another job to which your personality is well suited.

Smile! You're unique!

You're a product of your genes and your environment, and I can guarantee that you are unique. A personality scale with just 10 factors, using a standardised 10-point scoring scale on each factor, tells us that ten thousand million possible unique personality profiles exist. That's more people than live on planet Earth! And some personality scales run to 30 or more traits! You can see why choosing a specific profile and saying 'That's the candidate we want to find!' is a waste of time.

No one has the right to criticise or demand you make changes to your personality. Although you can go on training courses to find out how to behave in certain ways (for example, discovering how to make a presentation without sounding nervous), genuinely changing your personality so that you actually *are* less nervous is much harder.

Imagine that you applied for a job as a sales executive. This job requires you to travel around the county alone, meet clients, try to sell products, and arrange delivery of products to them. To be successful you must be self-reliant, assertive, socially confident, enthusiastic, and well-organised. Imagine how difficult the job would be if you are lower than most salespersons on any of these traits.

Telling the truth, and not answering the questions in a way that doesn't genuinely describe you, is very important in personality tests. If you manage to convince a recruiter that you are highly self-reliant, when in fact you're someone who needs social contact with other people to be happy, imagine how miserable you're going to be in the sales executive role.

Dealing with personality tests

For our purposes, we can consider two main approaches to measuring personality: *type* and *trait approaches*. They differ more in their views of the nature of personality than in their question formats. The number of questions in a personality test varies widely depending on the number of characteristics being measured and how the test designer chooses to view personality as being constructed. I have seen personality tests with as few as 40 items and as many as 400, although most seem to settle at 100–200 questions. The number of questions isn't generally anything to worry about because you're not normally placed under a time limit to complete them.

Examples of personality type tests

Type approaches argue that if you have a preference on one scale, it necessarily and unavoidably reduces your preference on the opposite scale. So, scoring highly on extroversion (the extent to which you are socially oriented) automatically produces a low score on introversion, and classifies you as an *extroverted type*.

This question is like asking, 'Which hand do you prefer using – your left hand or your right?' If you use your left hand 70 per cent of the time, you only use your right hand 30 per cent of the time.

Personality type questions allow you to choose between the characteristics of two types. The scoring then classifies you as the type for which you have the most responses. In allotting you to a type, the test takes no account of the difference between the scores on the two types.

Here are the style of questions you may come across in a personality type test:

1. Circle the word that most describes you:

i. (a) outgoing   *(b) shy*

ii. (a) assertive   *(b) co-operative*

2. I would rather read a book than go to a noisy party.

(a) agree   *(b) disagree*

Type tests are often very elegantly designed, and the type approach is very useful in individual and team development, but they aren't generally used in recruitment.

Examples of personality trait tests

Trait approaches view personality scales as being separate, and your score on one scale can vary independently of the other scale. So, these tests can recognise elements of both traits in your personality.

A trait approach question asks you how much you like using your right hand, and how much you like using your left.

Measuring the same characteristics as the type test examples in the previous section, a trait test may phrase its questions as follows:

1. Indicate whether you agree or disagree with the following descriptions of your personality:

i. outgoing *(a) agree* *(b) no preference* *(c) disagree*

ii. shy   *(a) agree* *(b) no preference* *(c) disagree*

iii. assertive   *(a) agree*   *(b) no preference*
(c) disagree

iv. co-operative *(a) agree*   *(b) no preference*
(c) disagree

2. I enjoy solitary hobbies.

(a) agree   *(b) no preference*   *(c) disagree*

3. I enjoy going to noisy parties.

(a) agree   *(b) no preference*   *(c) disagree*

The questions above all relate to *extroversion.* In a trait test like this, you can say that you enjoy solitary hobbies (suggesting a more introverted nature) and at the same time that you enjoy going to noisy parties (suggesting a more extroverted nature). An overall score in this case may suggest that you're half way along the extroversion scale, midway between extraversion and introversion; in other words, average as compared to most people.

Because trait approaches measure each scale independently, recruiters use them to compare your score with another person's score. Type approaches can't compare in that way.

Skip to the personality assessment sample test in Chapter 14, where you can draw up your own personality trait profile.

Approaching Personality Tests

You can view a personality test as being composed of a long list of interview questions. These interview questions, however, have been statistically screened to ensure that they are relevant, accurate, and free from bias. The fact that you need to do nothing (that's right – nothing at all!) to prepare yourself for a personality test is another bonus.

Consider these tips when working through a personality test:

✔ **Work fast.** The faster you work, the more accurate is your profile. If you spend one minute thinking about each question, a 180-item test takes 3 hours to complete!

✔ **Go with your gut instinct.** Your initial answer is probably the right one. If you take too long, you're thinking about your answer in too much detail.

✔ **Unless you're absolutely unsure, avoid using any 'don't know' options.** Try to mark a definite preference wherever possible.

✔ **Don't second-guess yourself.** Once you've answered a question honestly, don't go back and change it unless you're sure that you need to.

✔ **Don't worry if you think your answers to different questions about the same trait are contradictory.** Similar sounding questions are asked about a particular trait in a range of situations, and most people behave differently in one situation to another.

✔ **Tell the truth.** Misrepresenting yourself in order to get a job is dishonest, and can land you in a sticky situation later on – you may have to illustrate your profile with examples of actual behaviour during the feedback interview.

Part III

Getting Some Practise In: Sample Tests

'Before we start on the psychometric tests, I hope you're not feeling too nervous.'

In this part . . .

*G*et ready to start thinking, because in this part I give you some real tests to try – full-length versions of verbal, numerical, abstract, technical, and personality tests. You don't have to try the full-length versions if you don't want to. You may find it better just to dip quickly into each test and get a feel for the style of the questions.

The key to improving your chances of doing well on a psychometric test is to develop your underlying abilities by practising at a more reflective level. So, I've organised the chapters in this part to follow the same sequence as in Part II. This way, you can easily skip back to the relevant theory chapter if you want to know more about any particular test.

You're given a thousand questions in this part (really!). Please don't try them all in one go!

Chapter 10

Verbal Ability Sample Tests

● ●

In This Chapter

▶ Buzzing through spelling tests

▶ Grappling with grammar tests

▶ Considering comprehension tests

▶ Finding the answers

● ●

*E*mployers use verbal ability tests to assess how well you can use and understand language and solve word-based problems. This chapter gives you a range of verbal ability tests to try. You can just dip into a test, or try the whole thing using the time limits shown in Table 10–1.

Table 10–1   Verbal Ability Sample Test Time Limits

Type of Test	*Time Limit*
Spelling Speed Test	**20 minutes**
Spelling Power Test	**25 minutes**
Grammar Test	**25 minutes**
Comprehension Speed Tests	
Linking Words	20 minutes
Missing Words	20 minutes
Synonyms	20 minutes
Antonyms	20 minutes
Comprehension Power Test	**Untimed**

You can find the correct answers at the end of each test.

Spelling Speed Test

Your task in this spelling speed test is to identify the correct spelling from the list of words you are given. Circle your chosen answer.

1.	(a) garulous (b) garruless (c) garroulous (d) garrulous (e) none of them	**2.**	(a) mischievous (b) mischeivious (c) mischievious (d) mischievious (e) none of them
3.	(a) verascity (b) veraicity (c) verasity (d) verracity (e) none of them	**4.**	(a) entrepreneur (b) entrepreuner (c) entreprener (d) entrepruener (e) none of them
5.	(a) supercede (b) supersede (c) superceed (d) superscede (e) none of them	**6.**	(a) sucsession (b) succesion (c) sucession (d) succession (e) none of them
7.	(a) manouvre (b) manoeuver (c) maneuvre (d) manoeuvre (e) none of them	**8.**	(a) simultaneously (b) simultaneusly (c) similtaneously (d) simaltaneously (e) none of them
9.	(a) hypotinuse (b) hypotanuse (c) hypoteneuse (d) hypotenuse (e) none of them	**10.**	(a) choroegraph (b) chorreograph (c) choreograph (d) choreographe (e) none of them

11. (a) pronunciation
    (b) pronaunciation
    (c) pronanciation
    (d) pronuntiacion
    (e) none of them

12. (a) pharmaceutical
    (b) pharmaceutacil
    (c) pharmacutical
    (d) pharmacuetical
    (e) none of them

13. (a) idiosynchrasy
    (b) idiosyncracy
    (c) idiosynchracy
    (d) idosyncrasy
    (e) none of them

14. (a) facestious
    (b) fascetious
    (c) facecious
    (d) facetious
    (e) none of them

15. (a) harrass
    (b) harras
    (c) harase
    (d) harass
    (e) none of them

16. (a) bizzarre
    (b) bizarre
    (c) bizare
    (d) bizzare
    (e) none of them

17. (a) susceptible
    (b) suseptable
    (c) suceptible
    (d) susceptable
    (e) none of them

18. (a) omniescience
    (b) omnicience
    (c) omniscence
    (d) omniscience
    (e) none of them

19. (a) remembrance
    (b) rememberance
    (c) remmembrance
    (d) rememmbrance
    (e) none of them

20. (a) vaccum
    (b) vacum
    (c) vacuumm
    (d) vaccuum
    (e) none of them

21. (a) Fahrenheit
    (b) Farhenheit
    (c) Farehneit
    (d) Fahrenhite
    (e) none of them

22. (a) deviency
    (b) deveancy
    (c) deviancy
    (d) devianecy
    (e) none of them

23. (a) unanaimous
    (b) unaniamous
    (c) unanamous
    (d) unanimous
    (e) none of them

24. (a) hemorrhage
    (b) haemorrhage
    (c) haemorhage
    (d) haemorrage
    (e) none of them

25. (a) persevirance
(b) persaverance
(c) perserverance
(d) perseverance
(e) none of them

26. (a) acommodate
(b) accomodate
(c) acomodate
(d) accommodate
(e) none of them

27. (a) comemorate
(b) commemmorate
(c) commemorate
(d) commemerate
(e) none of them

28. (a) beginnings
(b) begginnings
(c) beginings
(d) begginings
(e) none of them

29. (a) presumptious
(b) presumptous
(c) presumtuous
(d) presumpcious
(e) none of them

30. (a) handkercheif
(b) hankerchief
(c) hankercheif
(d) handkerchief
(e) none of them

31. (a) embarassment
(b) embarrasment
(c) embarasment
(d) embarrassment
(e) none of them

32. (a) reconnaissance
(b) reconaissance
(c) reconnaisance
(d) reconaisance
(e) none of them

33. (a) indispensible
(b) indespensable
(c) indespensible
(d) indispensable
(e) none of them

34. (a) sacralegious
(b) sacraligious
(c) sacrilegious
(d) sacriligious
(e) none of them

35. (a) acidentaly
(b) acidentally
(c) accidentaly
(d) accidentally
(e) none of them

36. (a) milenium
(b) milennium
(c) millenium
(d) millennium
(e) none of them

37. (a) apparantly
(b) apparrantly
(c) aparently
(d) apparently
(e) none of them

38. (a) vendeta
(b) venndetta
(c) vendetta
(d) venndeta
(e) none of them

39. (a) miniaturisation (b) miniturisation (c) miniatarisation (d) minaturisation (e) none of them	**40.** (a) ocasionally (b) occasionaly (c) ocasionaly (d) occasionally (e) none of them
41. (a) noticable (b) noticible (c) noticeable (d) noticeble (e) none of them	**42.** (a) pronnunciation (b) pronunnciation (c) pronunciation (d) pronuntiation (e) none of them
43. (a) conveniantly (b) convenniently (c) conveniently (d) convieniently (e) none of them	**44.** (a) guarantee (b) guarauntee (c) guaranntee (d) guarrantee (e) none of them
45. (a) weird (b) weirrd (c) wierd (d) wierrd (e) none of them	**46.** (a) licquefaction (b) liquafaction (c) liquifaction (d) liquefaction (e) none of them
47. (a) apalling (b) appaling (c) appalling (d) appauling (e) none of them	**48.** (a) inheritability (b) inheritibility (c) innheritability (d) inheriatability (e) none of them
49. (a) illegitimat (b) ilegitamate (c) illegitimate (d) ilegitimate (e) none of them	**50.** (a) flabergasted (b) flabberghasted (c) flaberghasted (d) flabbergasted (e) none of them

Answers: 1. (d); **2.** (a); **3.** (e); **4.** (a); **5.** (b); **6.** (d); **7.** (d); **8.** (a); **9.** (d); **10.** (c); **11.** (a); **12.** (a); **13.** (e); **14.** (d); **15.** (d); **16.** (b); **17.** (a); **18.** (d); **19.** (a); **20.** (e); **21.** (a); **22.** (c); **23.** (d); **24.** (b); **25.** (d); **26.** (d); **27.** (c); **28** . (a); **29.** (e); **30.** (d); **31.** (d); **32.** (a); **33.** (d); **34.** (c); **35.** (d); **36.** (d); **37.** (d); **38.** (c); **39.** (a); **40.** (d); **41.** (c) **42.** (c); **43.** (c); **44.** (a); **45.** (a); **46.** (d); **47.** (c); **48.** (a); **49.** (c); **50.** (d).

Spelling Power Test

Your task in this spelling power test is to identify the incorrectly spelled word or words in each sentence. Underline those words from the answer options that you think are spelled incorrectly. If you think none of the words are spelled incorrectly then choose answer option (e). More than one word can be spelled incorrectly in each sentence.

1. The politicians looked listlesly around the celebratory proccesion.

(a) listlesly   (b) celebratory   (c) proccesion   (d) all correct

2. The sum of the internal angles in an equiliteral triangle (a type of isosceles triangle) is always 180 degrees.

(a) equiliteral   (b) isosceles   (c) angles   (d) all correct

3. Governments can only be effectively challenged in a parlamentary democracy.

(a) governments   (b) effectively   (c) parlamentary
(d) all correct

4. Suspicion fell on the vendor for peddling counterfiet merchandise.

(a) Suspicion   (b) peddling   (c) counterfiet   (d) all correct

5. Beautiful figurines are ornamental rather than functional.

(a) figurines   (b) ornamental   (c) functional   (d) all correct

6. Paddocks require effective fencing to keep horses from roaming.

(a) paddocks   (b) effective   (c) roaming   (d) all correct

7. The restaunaters are proud of their culinary reputations.

(a) restaunaters (b) culinary   (c) reputations   (d) all correct

8. A satisfactory night's sleep depends on no disfunction in circaidian rhythms.

(a) satisfactory (b) disfunction (c) circaidian (d) all correct

9. The bombadier couragously maintained position by his wounded comrade.

(a) bombadier (b) couragously (c) comrade (d) all correct

10. The proffessor was affable, intelligent, and knowlegeable.

(a) proffessor (b) intelligent (c) knowlegeable (d) all correct

11. The disturbance was unavoidable but dealt with by the marshals with profficiency.

(a) disturbance (b) marshals (c) profficiency (d) all correct

12. Reconnaissance suggested a reoccupation of the abandoned positions.

(a) Reconnaissance (b) reoccupation (c) abandoned
(d) all correct

13. To avoid aggrevating an old injury, try some rudimentary callisthenics as a prerequsite to exercise.

(a) aggrevating (b) prerequsite (c) callisthenics (d) all correct

14. Her introductory remarks were both informitave and disarmingly frank.

(a) introductory (b) informitave (c) disarmingly (d) all correct

15. The efficient running of the office neccesarily depended upon the accuracy of the requsitioning system.

(a) efficient (b) neccesarily (c) requsitioning (d) all correct

16. The stipendary magistrate may recommend a non-custodial sentence.

(a) stipendary (b) recommend (c) custodial (d) all correct

17. Gerrymandering is the division of constituancy boundries to maximise the votes for a particular political party.

(a) Gerrymandering (b) constituancy (c) boundries (d) all correct

18. The Egyptologists approached the sarchophagus with some trepedation and excitement.

(a) Egyptologists (b) sarchophagus (c) trepedation (d) all correct

19. The monotonous rhythm of the penduluum can have a soporiphic effect on the observer.

(a) monotonous (b) penduluum (c) soporiphic (d) all correct

20. Fire retardant materials are designed to be fire resistant rather than incombustable.

(a) retardant (b) resistant (c) incombustable (d) all correct

21. Birds that nest on stony beaches use camouflage so as to be inconspicuous.

(a) stony (b) camouflage (c) inconspicuous (d) all correct

22. The synchronisation of orchestral instruments produces a harmonious effect.

(a) synchronisation (b) orchestral (c) harmonious (d) all correct

23. Arithmetic proggresions involve many sequential numbers, which change according to a predictable rule.

(a) Arithmetic (b) proggresions (c) sequential (d) all correct

24. From atop the hill she could freely walk without hindrance or encumberance in any direction.

(a) atop (b) hindrance (c) encumberance (d) all correct

25. By meticulously studying ancient manuscripts it is often possible to place them in chronalogical order.

(a) meticulously (b) manuscripts (c) chronalogical (d) all correct

26. Numerous misellaneous artefacts were discovered during the investagative process.

(a) misellaneous (b) artefacts (c) investagative (d) all correct

27. The menagery of animals created a riotous cachophony of sound.

(a) menagery (b) riotous (c) cachophony (d) all correct

28. A reapprasal of the salient points in an argument may reveal some consequental impact on the parties involved.

(a) reapprasal (b) salient (c) consequental (d) all correct

29. The beneficary of a last will and testament may not also be an executor.

(a) beneficary (b) testament (c) executor (d) all correct

30. They heard many humourus mispronuncations in the discourse.

(a) humourus (b) mispronuncations (c) discourse (d) all correct

31. The Minotaur was a mythological creature with which a great deal of mystiqe has become associated.

(a) Minotaur (b) mystiqe (c) associated (d) all correct

32. The variability of sunspots, which are magnetic phenomena on the surface of the sun, can explain apparent changes in the luminosity of the sun over time.

(a) variability (b) phenomena (c) luminosity (d) all correct

33. The observer infers, whereas the observed implies. The difference between the two is often misunderstood.

(a) infers   (b) difference   (c) misunderstood   (d) all correct

34. The superintendant, also known as the building commisioner, is responsible for the repair and maintenance of the facility.

(a) superintendant   (b) commisioner   (c) maintenance   (d) all correct

35. The lack of any semblance of effective record keeping was tantamount to negligence.

(a) semblance   (b) tantamount   (c) negligence   (d) all correct

36. In the management heirarchy it was acknowledged that fischal planning fell under the remit of the finance director.

(a) heirarchy   (b) fischal   (c) remit   (d) all correct

37. The main protaganist devised an inginious technique to circumvent the usual rules and regulations.

(a) protaganist   (b) inginious   (c) technique   (d) all correct

38. The goverment at the time was especially concerned that the new legislation should send out a clear deterent message.

(a) goverment   (b) especially   (c) deterent   (d) all correct

39. He broke the ornament accidentaly, but his conscience was still causing him some angst.

(a) accidentaly   (b) conscience   (c) angst   (d) all correct

40. Even with a wide vocabulary, incorrect pronnunciation can be embarassing.

(a) vocabulary   (b) pronnunciation   (c) embarassing   (d) all correct

Answers: 1. (a) & (c); **2.** (a); **3.** (c); **4.** (c); **5.** (d); **6.** (d); **7.** (a); **8.** (b) & c); **9.** (a) & (b); **10.** (a) & (c); **11.** (c); **12.** (d); **13.** (a) & (b); **14.** (b); **15.** (b) & (c); **16.** (a); **17.** (b) & (c); **18.** (b) & (c); **19.** (b) & (c); **20.** (c); **21.** (d); **22.** (d); **23.** (b); **24.** (c); **25.** (c); **26.** (a), & (c); **27.** (a) & (c); **28.** (a) & (c); **29.** (a); **30.** (a) & (b); **31.** (b); **32.** (d); **33.** (d); **34.** (a) & (b); **35.** (d); **36.** (a) & (b); **37.** (a) & (b); **38.** (a) & (c); **39.** (a); **40.** (b) & (c).

Grammar Test

Your task in this grammar test is to write down the grammatically correct version of each statement. If you think the statement already is grammatically correct, write 'correct'.

1. Its going to be sunny tomorrow.

_____

2. He doesn't live here no more.

_____

3. The men worked hard all day.

_____

4. It doesn't have to be arranged that way.

_____

5. I think that dog has lost its owner.

_____

6. He has took the bus to school three time this week.

_____

7. I would of done it but I didn't have the time.

_____

8. Don't worry, I done it yesterday.

_____

9. Please don't do that no more.

_____

10. After I locked myself out I tried for an hour to get in the house.

_____

11. The picture is the one of us on holiday.

_____

12. It's not possible anymore to work those hours.

_____

13. It's a hard lesson to learn.

_____

14. I seen him yesterday, he didn't look very happy.

_____

15. The parcel's will be ready for collection tomorrow.

_____

16. I like the colour of that jacket, I'm going to try it on.

_____

17. Your the funniest people I have ever met!

_____

18. Don't forget to collect them people tonight.

_____

19. It's true, and it has always been true.

_____

20. It don't always matter if you're late.

_____

21. Its been done before.

_____

22. Look, over their – did you see it?

_____

23. You didn't park you're car very well did you!

_____

24. Give them there dues, they stuck to the task in hand.

_____

25. I write good, and draw much better.

_____

26. The experience had a strange affect on me.

_____

27. The dog slept soundly in it's basket.

_____

28. The crowd are angry.

_____

29. They were the ones that built the first bridge.

_____

30. To who are you referring?

_____

Answers (if a sentence isn't listed here, it was grammatically correct already): 1. It's going to be sunny tomorrow. **2.** He doesn't live here any more. **6.** He has taken the bus to school three times this week. **7.** I would have done it but I didn't have the time. **8.** Don't worry, I did it yesterday. **9.** Please don't do that any more. **10.** After I locked myself out I tried for an hour to get into the house. **12.** It's no longer possible to work those hours. **14.** I saw him yesterday, he didn't look very happy. **15.** The parcels will be ready for collection tomorrow. **16.** I like the colour of that jacket, and I'm going to try it on. **17.** You're the funniest people I have ever met! **18.** Don't forget to collect those people tonight. **20.** It doesn't always matter if you're late. **21.** It's been done before. **22.** Look, over there – did you see it? **23.** You didn't park your car very well did you! **24.** Give them their dues, they stuck to the task in hand. **25.** I write well, and draw much better. **26.** The experience had a strange effect on me. **27.** The dog slept soundly in its basket. **28.** The crowd is angry. **29.** They were the ones who built the first bridge. **30.** To whom are you referring?

Comprehension Speed Tests

The tests in this section assess how well you understand, and can work with, words and sentences.

Linking words

In this comprehension speed test you need to choose the word from the answer options that joins both words given in the question to form two new phrases. The correct answers follow the test.

1. hat _____ shot

(a) stand   (b) slap   (c) hit   (d) trick

2. alarm _____ watching

(a) bell   (b) clock   (c) bird   (d) time

3. head _____ bulb

(a) light   (b) lice   (c) car   (d) hat

4. home _____ camera

(a) safe   (b) digital   (c) video   (d) run

5. air _____ calculator

(a) gun   (b) passage   (c) horn   (d) pocket

6. church _____ way

(a) tower   (b) hall   (c) right   (d) high

7. battle _____ shape

(a) ship   (b) hard   (c) loose   (d) round

8. sea _____ style

(a) side   (b) life   (c) free   (d) lion

9. hard _____ stand

(a) head   (b) hat   (c) top   (d) last

10. olive _____ slick

(a) paint   (b) smooth   (c) oil   (d) tan

11. spare _____ barrow

(a) wheel   (b) change   (c) down   (d) trench

12. air _____ shaft

(a) lift   (b) tight   (c) mine   (d) light

13. hobby _____ riding

(a) game   (b) horse   (c) night   (d) bike

14. bed _____ out

(a) frame   (b) time   (c) night   (d) sheet

15. summer _____ maker

(a) sun   (b) bread   (c) holiday   (d) time

16. north _____ lion

(a) sea   (b) south   (c) pole   (d) Africa

17. open _____ station

(a) space   (b) world   (c) train   (d) office

18. pet _____ chain

(a) name   (b) link   (c) food   (d) dog

19. tree _____ boat

(a) house   (b) narrow   (c) leaf   (d) top

20. royal _____ fish

(a) crown   (b) occasion   (c) star   (d) jelly

21. sticky _____ recorder

(a) spot   (b) times   (c) label   (d) tape

22. planet _____ worm

(a) sun   (b) earth   (c) hole   (d) sea

23. sun _____ square

(a) set   (b) spot   (c) angle   (d) down

24. south _____ star

(a) north   (b) pole   (c) end   (d) rising

25. high _____ mark

(a) life   (b) tide   (c) top   (d) roller

26. snow _____ **front**

(a) cloud   (b) warm   (c) storm   (d) cold

27. air _____ **affairs**

(a) current   (b) private   (c) war   (d) warm

28. cliff _____ **hat**

(a) bowler   (b) edge   (c) down   (d) top

29. junior _____ **uniform**

(a) school   (b) clean   (c) senior   (d) janitor

30. car _____ **basin**

(a) port   (b) sink   (c) wash   (d) keys

31. super _____ **garden**

(a) store   (b) back   (c) nova   (d) market

32. pitch _____ **hole**

(a) tar   (b) black   (c) worm   (d) throw

33. rally _____ **purposes**

(a) sport   (b) my   (c) cross   (d) gathering

34. lunch _____ **zone**

(a) time   (b) end   (c) meat   (d) food

35. key _____ **game**

(a) stone   (b) end   (c) board   (d) chain

36. rain _____ **colour**

(a) water   (b) wet   (c) paint   (d) cloud

37. magic _____ **buoy**

(a) show   (b) life   (c) marker   (d) trick

38. story _____ **end**

(a) time   (b) book   (c) life   (d) lands

39. back _____ **horse**

(a) cart   (b) pack   (c) basic   (d) shire

40. head _____ **meeting**

(a) board   (b) emergency   (c) master   (d) boy

Answers: 1. (d); **2.** (b); **3.** (a); **4.** (c); **5.** (d); **6.** (b); **7.** (a); **8.** (b); **9.** (b); **10.** (c); **11.** (a); **12.** (a); **13.** (b); **14.** (b); **15.** (c); **16.** (a); **17.** (a); **18.** (c); **19.** (a); **20.** (d); **21.** (d); **22.** (b); **23.** (a); **24.** (b); **25.** (b); **26.** (c); **27.** (a); **28.** (d); **29.** (a); **30.** (c); **31.** (d); **32.** (b); **33.** (c); **34.** (a); **35.** (c); **36.** (a); **37.** (c); **38.** (b); **39.** (b); **40.** (a).

Missing words

This second comprehension speed test asks you to complete each sentence using one of the words you are given. Often, more than one of the answer options fits, but you need to choose which one makes the most sense. Circle your chosen answer.

1. Finding on-street parking is becoming increasingly _____.

(a) difficult   (b) scarce   (c) common   (d) harder

2. The price of a top of the range computer _____ **to stay about same.**

(a) never   (b) always   (c) tends   (d) expensive

3. The 24 hour system of time is used more _____ **in mainland Europe than in the UK.**

(a) less   (b) commonly   (c) easy   (d) accurate

4. Grass grows more slowly _____ the winter months.

(a) because   (b) during   (c) especially   (d) stops

5. A round trip to London is a _____ way to drive in a single day.

(a) wise   (b) good   (c) long   (d) usual

6. The earliest age at which one can leave school is 16 years _____.

(a) time   (b) away   (c) ago   (d) old

7. Christmas just seems to get more _____ every year.

(a) cheaper   (b) less   (c) snow   (d) expensive

8. Cooking is a hobby which many people _____.

(a) bake   (b) prepare   (c) cook   (d) enjoy

9. It's only fair that neighbours who share a garden must take _____ mowing the lawn.

(a) chances   (b) initiative   (c) care   (d) turns

10. One has a choice of using _____ metric or imperial weights when purchasing goods.

(a) the   (b) often   (c) either   (d) neither

11. Speed _____ are there for the safety of all road users and should be observed by all.

(a) limits   (b) bumps   (c) cars   (d) cameras

12. These days there is very little one cannot _____ out by conducting research on the Internet.

(a) do   (b) look   (c) find   (d) go

13. On average people change jobs _____ four or five years.

(a) every   (b) once   (c) sometimes (d) try

14. In 1987 red was the most _____ colour of car, in 2004 it was silver.

(a) often   (b) popular   (c) nicest   (d) bright

15. Most children can tell the time by _____ the age of six or seven.

(a) clock   (b) looking   (c) about   (d) practice

16. More _____ are recycling their domestic waste these days.

(a) businesses (b) councils (c) people   (d) bin

17. Employability is enhanced by educational _____.

(a) work   (b) time   (c) thought   (d) qualifications

18. Scientists who work near the summits of volcanoes have to wear heat _____ suits for protection.

(a) resistant (b) tolerant   (c) cooling   (d) powered

19. I would rather hire a decorator than paint an entire _____ myself.

(a) front   (b) build   (c) day   (d) house

20. The football season starts a week _____ in Scotland than it does in England.

(a) after   (b) earlier   (c) shorter   (d) because

21. Triggered by a drop in _____, most trees lose their leaves in autumn.

(a) birds   (b) seeds   (c) temperature (d) daylight

22. Dinosaurs lived millions of years before _____ humans appeared on earth.

(a) us   (b) people   (c) species   (d) modern

23. It is possible to fly from London to New York in just a few _____ .

(a) hours   (b) parties   (c) planes   (d) times

24. Pulley systems are use by builders to help them lift _____ loads.

(a) your   (b) house   (c) pallet   (d) heavy

25. Generally, the larger a vehicle's engine capacity, the fewer miles it will _____ per litre of fuel.

(a) consume   (b) motor   (c) travel   (d) power

26. Modern trains are powered by electricity, delivered by _____ of an overhead wire.

(a) men   (b) means   (c) cables   (d) power

27. Pencils are made from a core of clay and graphite sandwiched between two _____ of wood.

(a) pieces   (b) planks   (c) trees   (d) sticks

28. Before washing machines were invented everyone had to wash their _____ by hand.

(a) loads   (b) works   (c) machines   (d) clothes

29. The Eiffel tower in Paris is one of the most _____ structures in Europe.

(a) beautiful   (b) straightest   (c) oldest   (d) tallest

30. Water increases in _____ when it is frozen.

(a) ice   (b) temperature   (c) volume   (d) freezing

31. Wood does not _____ electricity.

(a) conduct   (b) burn   (c) stop   (d) allow

32. If dropped into water an object will always _____ an amount of water equal to its own volume.

(a) wash (b) spill (c) float (d) displace

33. There are thousands of languages spoken in the _____.

(a) world (b) book (c) school (d) future

34. Niagara falls are located on the _____ between the US and Canada.

(a) gap (b) waterfall (c) border (d) site

35. Solar, tidal, and wind power _____ be used to generate electricity.

(a) all (b) often (c) can (d) never

36. Most pearls we see today are artificial. Genuine pearls are _____ inside oysters.

(a) made (b) living (c) grit (d) laid

37. Science can be defined more in _____ of its processes than its outcomes.

(a) terms (b) words (c) theories (d) scientists

38. Many medicines are based on chemical _____ first discovered in plants.

(a) materials (b) compounds (c) ideas (d) atoms

39. Ludwig van Beethoven was one of the world's _____ composers.

(a) piano (b) last (c) first (d) greatest

40. The great wall of China is visible from _____.

(a) there (b) beneath (c) tower (d) space

41. You do not have to be _____ to play sport, however being physically fit will help.

(a) athlete   (b) tall   (c) fit   (d) keen

42. Some fruits and vegetables are harder to _____ during the winter months, but most are still available.

(a) eat   (b) obtain   (c) cook   (d) peel

43. Despite playing well the team still _____ the match.

(a) abandoned   (b) won   (c) lost   (d) struck

44. She walked her _____ every day without fail.

(a) preferred   (b) dog   (c) self   (d) friend

45. Restoring old cars is a challenging but _____ expensive hobby.

(a) somewhat   (b) happily   (c) bodywork   (d) technical

46. It is important to read the _____ before attempting to operate any new kitchen appliances.

(a) instructions   (b) small print   (c) contract   (d) receipt

47. Every month he checked his pay slip _____ to ensure that he had been paid for his overtime.

(a) once   (b) sometimes   (c) carefully   (d) quietly

48. Most candidates are rather _____ before job interviews.

(a) checked   (b) late   (c) coffee   (d) nervous

49. I have never met anybody who manages to get eight hours of _____ a night.

(a) exercise   (b) kids   (c) sleep   (d) play

50. A well _____ revision schedule is the key to exam success.

(a) drawn   (b) careful   (c) rigid   (d) planned

Answers: 1. (a); **2.** (c); **3.** (b); **4.** (b); **5.** (c); **6.** (d); **7.** (d); **8.** (d); **9.** (d); **10.** (c); **11.** (a); **12.** (c); **13.** (a); **14.** (b); **15.** (c); **16.** (c); **17.** (d); **18.** (a); **19.** (d); **20.** (b); **21.** (c); **22.** (d); **23.** (a); **24.** (d); **25.** (c); **26.** (b); **27.** (a); **28.** (d); **29.** (a); **30.** (c); **31.** (a); **32.** (d); **33.** (a); **34.** (c); **35.** (c); **36.** (a); **37.** (a); **38.** (b); **39.** (d); **40.** (d); **41.** (d); **42.** (b); **43.** (c); **44.** (b); **45.** (a); **46.** (a); **47.** (c); **48.** (d); **49.** (c); **50.** (d).

Synonyms

This third comprehension speed test asks you to look at *synonyms* (words with the same meaning). Circle your chosen answer.

1. What means the same as adduce?

(a) cite   (b) deduce   (c) infer   (d) imply

2. What means the same as fortuitous?

(a) lucky   (b) chance   (c) strong   (d) wilful

3. What means the same as negation?

(a) cancellation   (b) negative   (c) criticism   (d) change

4. What means the same as amalgam?

(a) split   (b) alloy   (c) metal   (d) combination

5. What means the same as insinuate?

(a) ingratiate   (b) accuse   (c) stretch   (d) imply

6. What means the same as vestibule?

(a) boil   (b) carbuncle   (c) lobby   (d) priest

7. What means the same as unanimity?

(a) hostility   (b) disagree   (c) single   (d) accord

8. What means the same as blithe?

(a) bleached (b) faded   (c) casual   (d) damp

9. What means the same as supposition?

(a) oppose   (b) position   (c) argument   (d) assumption

10. What means the same as eulogise?

(a) extol   (b) lecture   (c) apologise   (d) write

11. What means the same as interdict?

(a) intervene (b) criticise   (c) prohibit   (d) cancel

12. What means the same as disquiet?

(a) displease (b) silent   (c) loud   (d) unease

13. What means the same as burnish?

(a) shine   (b) alight   (c) burn   (d) gleaming

14. What means the same as pugnacious?

(a) boxing   (b) fighter   (c) argumentative (d) stupid

15. What means the same as meagre?

(a) cruel   (b) meal   (c) thin   (d) paltry

16. What means the same as invidious?

(a) inseparable (b) jealous   (c) unpleasant (d) envious

17. What means the same as fusion?

(a) heat   (b) boiling   (c) fission   (d) union

18. What means the same as cutlass?

(a) compass (b) sword   (c) dagger   (d) sextant

19. What means the same as martinet?

(a) hen   (b) disciplinarian   (c) officer   (d) soldier

20. What means the same as promulgate?

(a) disperse (b) plant   (c) announce   (d) diversify

21. What means the same as placate?

(a) pacify   (b) slide   (c) stack   (d) panel

22. What means the same as overwrought?

(a) tense   (b) ironwork   (c) smelted   (d) heavy

23. What means the same as monologue?

(a) homogenous   (b) breed   (c) cat   (d) speech

24. What means the same as idiosyncrasy?

(a) silly   (b) habit   (c) foible   (d) technology

25. What means the same as ominous?

(a) entire   (b) worry   (c) foreboding (d) entirety

26. What means the same as moniker?

(a) name   (b) eyeglass   (c) telescope   (d) talent

27. What means the same as sonnet?

(a) story   (b) poem   (c) tale   (d) song

28. What means the same as repository?

(a) church   (b) repast   (c) returning   (d) depot

29. What means the same as capricious?

(a) tenacious (b) childish   (c) pretty   (d) impulsive

30. What means the same as intangible?

(a) insubstantial (b) tangential (c) unclear (d) opaque

31. What means the same as missive?

(a) concealment (b) letter   (c) discourse (d) ignore

32. What means the same as eke?

(a) thin   (b) starve   (c) increase   (d) eat

33. What means the same as bipartite?

(a) bipedal   (b) political   (c) dual   (d) partisan

34. What means the same as bespoke?

(a) wheel   (b) wooden   (c) custom   (d) sewn

35. What means the same as scathing?

(a) critical   (b) marking   (c) scouring   (d) boiling

36. What means the same as annul?

(a) cancel   (b) yearly   (c) record   (d) book

37. What means the same as prudence?

(a) meanness (b) caution   (c) focussed   (d) tightly

38. What means the same as reciprocal?

(a) revolving (b) mutual   (c) rotating   (d) swapping

39. What means the same as interim?

(a) trainee   (b) incarcerate (c) temporary (d) medic

40. What means the same as falsity?

(a) lie   (b) dentures   (c) truth   (d) disbelief

41. What means the same as inane?

(a) senseless   (b) boring   (c) sterile   (d) imprisoned

42. What means the same as scarper?

(a) scrape   (b) run   (c) steal   (d) fleeing

43. What means the same as peculate?

(a) muscular   (b) risk   (c) save   (d) embezzle

44. What means the same as outmoded?

(a) old   (b) surpassed   (c) slow   (d) unfashionable

45. What means the same as haughty?

(a) tight   (b) arrogant   (c) tied   (d) humorous

46. What means the same as salient?

(a) salty   (b) striking   (c) incline   (d) released

47. What means the same as duplicity?

(a) deception   (b) double   (c) play   (d) lying

48. What means the same as brazen?

(a) hearth   (b) angry   (c) shameless   (d) fire

49. What means the same as insular?

(a) lonely   (b) island   (c) isolated   (d) internal

50. What means the same as hawser?

(a) rope   (b) ship   (c) boat   (d) net

Answers: 1. (a); **2.** (b); **3.** (a); **4.** (d); **5.** (d); **6.** (c); **7.** (d); **8.** (c); **9.** (d); **10.** (a); **11.** (c); **12.** (d); **13.** (a); **14.** (c); **15.** (d); **16.** (c); **17.** (d); **18.** (b); **19.** (b); **20.** (c); **21.** (a); **22.** (a); **23.** (d); **24.** (c); **25.** (c); **26.** (a); **27.** (b); **28.** (d); **29.** (d); **30.** (a); **31.** (b); **32.** (c); **33.** (d); **34.** (c); **35.** (a); **36.** (a); **37.** (b); **38.** (b); **39.** (c); **40.** (a); **41.** (a); **42.** (b); **43.** (d); **44.** (d); **45.** (b); **46.** (b); **47.** (a); **48.** (c); **49.** (c); **50.** (a).

Antonyms

This fourth comprehension speed test asks you to look at *antonyms* (words with opposite meanings). Circle your chosen answer.

1. What is the opposite of subtle?

(a) obviate   (b) obvious   (c) large   (d) loud

2. What is the opposite of reduction?

(a) dilution   (b) increase   (c) enlarge   (d) larger

3. What is the opposite of opening?

(a) doorway   (b) vent   (c) closing   (d) door

4. What is the opposite of cooling?

(a) warming   (b) colder   (c) hot   (d) warmer

5. What is the opposite of destroyed?

(a) repaired   (b) damage   (c) rebuilt   (d) created

6. What is the opposite of sound?

(a) silence   (b) peace   (c) silent   (d) whisper

7. What is the opposite of flexible?

(a) adaptable   (b) rigid   (c) stiffly   (d) immovable

8. What is the opposite of alluring?

(a) captivating (b) repellent   (c) attractive (d) repulse

9. What is the opposite of return?

(a) keep   (b) retained   (c) departure (d) outward

10. What is the opposite of preference?

(a) choice   (b) either   (c) indifference (d) choose

11. What is the opposite of growing?

(a) shrinking   (b) detracting (c) expanding (d) smaller

12. What is the opposite of reserved?

(a) booked   (b) outgoing (c) kept   (d) freedom

13. What is the opposite of noticed?

(a) unclear   (b) noticeable (c) overlooked (d) notified

14. What is the opposite of proven?

(a) tested   (b) untrue   (c) tried   (d) untested

15. What is the opposite of satisfied?

(a) dissatisfaction (b) happy (c) discontent (d) discontented

16. What is the opposite of advocate?

(a) argue   (b) accept   (c) opponent (d) oppose

17. What is the opposite of scrupulous?

(a) sloppy   (b) lazy   (c) trustworthy (d) imprecise

18. What is the opposite of identified?

(a) unknown   (b) identity   (c) anonymous (d) unseen

19. What is the opposite of denied?

(a) admit   (b) allowed   (c) admittance (d) allowing

20. What is the opposite of changing?

(a) permanent (b) predictable (c) stability (d) stable

21. What is the opposite of conform?

(a) mutinous (b) loose (c) rebel (d) fit

22. What is the opposite of convivial?

(a) cool (b) generous (c) rejected (d) hostile

23. What is the opposite of lessen?

(a) increasing (b) decrease (c) less (d) increase

24. What is the opposite of abandon?

(a) located (b) reckless (c) keep (d) value

25. What is the opposite of opulent?

(a) ungracious (b) impoverished (c) tatty (d) lavish

26. What is the opposite of adulate?

(a) criticise (b) praise (c) grow (d) age

27. What is the opposite of success?

(a) triumph (b) achievement (c) victory (d) failure

28. What is the opposite of proficient?

(a) lacklustre (b) amateur (c) incompetent (d) lazy

29. What is the opposite of deliberate?

(a) accidental (b) consider (c) thoughtless (d) debate

30. What is the opposite of disband?

(a) unite (b) disharmonise (c) split (d) joined

31. What is the opposite of tardy?

(a) polish   (b) punctual   (c) shine   (d) improved

32. What is the opposite of rudimentary?

(a) complex   (b) simple   (c) basic   (d) single

33. What is the opposite of burden?

(a) work   (b) light   (c) relieve   (d) rest

34. What is the opposite of excess?

(a) shortage   (b) surfeit   (c) lessen   (d) less

35. What is the opposite of minimal?

(a) tiny   (b) most   (c) animal   (d) least

36. What is the opposite of soften?

(a) bake   (b) tougher   (c) malleable (d) harden

37. What is the opposite of denounce?

(a) criticise   (b) laudable   (c) praise   (d) noteworthy

38. What is the opposite of advance?

(a) retard   (b) backward (c) towards   (d) away

39. What is the opposite of immense?

(a) decreased   (b) tiny   (c) submerge (d) handheld

40. What is the opposite of futile?

(a) wasted   (b) pointless   (c) worthwhile (d) practical

41. What is the opposite of truthful?

(a) benign   (b) honesty   (c) liar   (d) dishonest

42. What is the opposite of secrete?

(a) hide   (b) open   (c) absorb   (d) adsorb

43. What is the opposite of collect?

(a) sow   (b) throw   (c) disperse   (d) gather

44. What is the opposite of break?

(a) cease   (b) combine   (c) repair   (d) snap

45. What is the opposite of tolerate?

(a) admonish   (b) venerate   (c) accept   (d) forbid

46. What is the opposite of approach?

(a) road   (b) retreat   (c) wait   (d) avoid

47. What is the opposite of opposite?

(a) mirror   (b) different   (c) same   (d) identical

48. What is the opposite of contempt?

(a) admiration   (b) dislike   (c) enjoyment   (d) assist

49. What is the opposite of heal?

(a) wound   (b) toe   (c) improve   (d) cure

50. What is the opposite of constant?

(a) variable   (b) regular   (c) moving   (d) static

Answers: 1. (b); **2.** (b); **3.** (c); **4.** (a); **5.** (d); **6.** (a); **7.** (b); **8.** (b); **9.** (c); **10.** (c); **11.** (a); **12.** (b); **13.** (c); **14.** (d); **15.** (d); **16.** (c); **17.** (a); **18.** (a); **19.** (b); **20.** (d); **21.** (c); **22.** (d); **23.** (d); **24.** (c); **25.** (b); **26.** (a); **27.** (d); **28.** (c); **29.** (a); **30.** (a); **31.** (b); **32.** (a); **33.** (c); **34.** (a); **35.** (b); **36.** (d); **37.** (c); **38.** (a); **39.** (b); **40.** (c); **41.** (d); **42.** (c); **43.** (c); **44.** (c); **45.** (d); **46.** (b); **47.** (c); **48.** (a); **49.** (a); **50.** (a).

Comprehension Power Test

In this comprehension power test, read each of the following five passages and the statements that follow each.

You need to decide whether each statement is true (based on what you've read), false (based on what you've read), or whether what you've read doesn't provide enough information to answer one way or the other.

Base your answers only on the information you read in the passages and statements. The information you are given may not be an accurate or a true reflection of the real world.

If you decide that a statement is true write 'T' to the left of the statement. For false write 'F' to the left of the statement. If you think it's impossible to say then write 'I' to the left of the statement.

1. Southern Elephant Seals

The population of the Southern Elephant Seal is probably less than a million worldwide. They are found in the cold Southern Ocean, where they spend most of their lives, and only come ashore to breed or moult. The largest known population can be found on the island of South Georgia.

Females reach sexual maturity much more quickly than males, and typically suckle their young for three or four weeks before leaving them to fend for themselves. Males are larger than females and can grow to lengths of up to twenty feet.

Elephant seals can dive to an astonishing one and a half miles and travel widely, often up to several thousand miles.

___ (a) Southern Elephant Seals are present in the northern hemisphere.

___ (b) fewer Southern Elephant Seals exist now than 100 years ago.

___ (c) the Southern Ocean is warming.

___ (d) Southern Elephant Seals have more than one cub at a time.

___ (e) Southern Elephant Seals breed in the ocean.

___ (f) female Southern Elephant Seals mature more quickly than males.

___ (g) male Southern Elephant Seals take an active part in rearing the young.

___ (h) female Southern Elephant Seals care for their young for up to a year.

___ (i) Southern Elephant Seals can dive to surprising depths.

___ (j) Southern Elephant Seals come ashore to moult.

___ (k) Southern Elephant Seals spend their lives on South Georgia.

___ (l) young Southern Elephant Seals are suckled for up to a month.

___ (m) female Southern Elephant Seals do not grow as large as males.

___ (n) male Southern Elephant Seals can grow to over 20 feet in length.

2. The Windscale Nuclear Accident

The Windscale nuclear accident happened in October 1957. A fire, the result of fuel rods overheating in the reactor core, was discovered on the 10th, although it must have been burning for up to 48 hours. At its peak, the temperature within the reactor chamber reached 1300 degrees Celsius.

After several unsuccessful attempts to extinguish the fire, it was finally put out on the 11th October by flooding the reactor chamber with water. It remains Britain's worst nuclear accident.

___ (a) the fire started on the 10th of October.

___ (b) initially the fire could not be put out.

___ (c) the Windscale nuclear accident happened in the latter half of 1957.

___ (d) the fire started before the 10th of October.

___ (e) the temperature within the fire reached 1300 degrees Celsius.

___ (f) the Windscale nuclear accident is the UK's worst ever nuclear accident.

___ (g) carbon dioxide was used to try and extinguish the fire.

___ (h) water put the fire out.

___ (i) putting the fire out took 3 days.

___ (j) the reactor chamber was a dangerous place to be during the fire.

___ (k) fuel rods were present in the reactor core.

___ (l) there was an inquiry after the fire.

___ (m) lots of people fought the fire.

___ (n) the fire was extinguished on the 11th October.

3. The History of the Euro

The Euro is the official currency of the European Union. Countries which use the Euro include Spain, France, Germany, Ireland, and Italy. The UK has not adopted the Euro as a single currency, although many UK businesses will accept it as a method of payment.

The Euro was introduced in 1999, but banknotes and coins were not issued until 2002. It is managed by the European Central Bank in Frankfurt. All EU member states who meet certain monetary requirements can join the Euro, but not all EU members have chosen to do so, even though they meet the requirements. There are more than 600 Billion Euro in circulation.

___ (a) the UK will adopt the Euro in 2012.

___ (b) the European Central Bank is in Germany.

___ (c) some EU members do not want to join the Euro.

___ (d) the Euro is a better investment than the dollar.

___ (e) the Euro was introduced in 2002.

___ (f) there are Euro notes and coins.

___ (g) there are 600 Billion Euro in circulation.

___ (h) all UK businesses accept the Euro as payment.

___ (i) the Euro is the official currency of the EU.

___ (j) the plural of Euro is Euro.

___ (k) the ECU was the predecessor of the Euro.

___ (l) UK businesses pay in Euro.

___ (m) one Euro is worth less than one UK Pound Sterling.

___ (n) the Euro is issued by the European Central Bank.

4. Water Abstraction

The process of taking water from any natural source, such as a river or reservoir, is known as *water abstraction*. Water taken in this way can be used for producing water for domestic uses such as drinking or washing, or can be used for irrigating farm land.

Water abstraction is regulated by law, and the amount of water that can be removed is strictly controlled. Too much abstraction from a single source can lead to a fall in river levels, or perhaps more seriously, a lowering of the underground water table.

___ (a) water abstraction reduces river levels.

___ (b) water abstraction is illegal.

___ (c) the underground water table is falling.

___ (d) domestic uses for water include drinking or washing.

___ (e) people use too much water.

___ (f) all farmers need to irrigate their fields.

___ (g) farmers need to provide water for their livestock.

___ (h) a lowering of the underground water table is serious.

___ (i) anyone can abstract water.

___ (j) it's better to abstract water from more than one source.

___ (k) farms use more water than domestic premises.

___ (l) crops get enough water from rainfall.

___ (m) drinking water needs to be treated.

___ (n) animals can drink rainwater.

5. Formative and Summative Evaluation

Two common practices in software development are formative evaluation and summative evaluation. Formative evaluation goes on before any actual software writing has been carried out, and involves evaluating the proposed software on paper, or perhaps using some non-functioning user interfaces to find the errors that usually exist, and assess how people understand and interact with the software in question.

Summative evaluation goes on after the software has been written and can go on for the whole lifespan of the software. Formative evaluation is cheaper to do because mistakes discovered during this stage are usually a lot easier and cheaper to correct than those discovered during the summative evaluation phase. This is mainly because the latter involves recalling software already in use.

___ (a) you have to develop trial interfaces when developing software.

___ (b) formative evaluation is hard to do.

___ (c) fixing errors found during summative evaluation is cheaper.

___ (d) all software development involves summative evaluation.

___ (e) software errors are usually found.

___ (f) software is harder to develop now than ten years ago.

___ (g) correcting errors found during summative evaluation is cheaper.

___ (h) software developers look at how well people understand software.

___ (i) most software is written for business use.

___ (j) formative evaluation is cheaper to carry out than summative evaluation.

___ (k) you can develop software without any evaluation.

___ (l) summative evaluation occurs after formative evaluation.

___ (m) formative evaluation is harder to do than summative evaluation.

___ (n) writing software is a complex task.

Answers: Comprehension power tests are one of the hardest types of test to complete. Scrutinise the wording and grammar of the sentence carefully if you don't agree with any of these answers. Subtle differences in meaning exist, and this test is designed to measure your ability to spot them.

1. Southern Elephant Seals

(a) I; (b) I; (c) I; (d) I; (e) F; (f) T; (g) I; (h) F; (i) T; (j) T; (k) F; (l) T; (m) T; (n) F.

2. The Windscale Nuclear Accident

(a) F; (b) T; (c) T; (d) T; (e) T; (f) T; (g) I; (h) T; (i) F; (j) T; (k) T; (l) I; (m) I; (n) T.

3. The History of the Euro

(a) I; (b) T; (c) T; (d) I; (e) F; (f) T; (g) F; (h) F; (i) T; (j) T; (k) I; (l) I; (m) I; (n) T.

4. Water Abstraction

(a) I; (b) F; (c) I; (d) T; (e) I; (f) I; (g) I; (h) T; (i) F; (j) T; (k) I; (l) F; (m) I; (n) I.

5. Formative and Summative Evaluation

(a) I; (b) I; (c) F; (d) I; (e) T; (f) I; (g) F; (h) T; (i) I; (j) T; (k) T; (l) T; (m) I; (n) I.

Chapter 11

Numerical Ability Sample Tests

. . . .

In This Chapter

▶ Giving your mathematical brain a workout

▶ Testing your numerical ability skills

▶ Checking out the answers

. . . .

*R*eassuringly, numerical tests are often easier than you
expect them to be, and here's your chance to get some
practice in. Even if you're about to face some higher level
numerical ability tests in real life, I suggest starting off with
the easier numerical ability tests to familiarise yourself with
some basic mathematical principles. Many people forget how
to do even basic maths when they're out of practice!

You can just answer a few sample questions, or take the plunge
and try the full version of each test. For the full versions, I suggest keeping to the time limits shown in Table 11–1.

Table 11–1	Numerical Ability and Reasoning Sample Test Time Limits
Type of Test	*Time Limit*
Numerical Ability Speed Test	**25 minutes**
Numerical Ability Power Test	**30 minutes**
Numerical Reasoning Speed Test	**30 minutes**
Numerical Reasoning Power Test	**Untimed**

You can find the correct answers at the end of each test.

Numerical Ability Speed Test

Your task in this numerical ability speed test is to work out what the question mark stands for, and to choose the correct answer from the options provided. Don't be tempted to use a calculator – that defeats the object of the test.

1. 5 + 8 + 5 + 5 = ?

(a) 18   (b) 21   (c) 23   (d) 25

2. 1 × 2 × 5 = ?

(a) 10   (b) 5   (c) 12   (d) 2

3. 72 + 8 - 8 - 11 = ?

(a) 70   (b) 72   (c) 78   (d) 61

4. 3 × 5 × 9 × 2 = ?

(a) 170   (b) 270   (c) 220   (d) 229

5. 6 + 22 - 19 + 5 = ?

(a) 28   (b) 29   (c) 14   (d) 17

6. 30 + 55 + 105 - 25 = ?

(a) 165   (b) 145   (c) 155   (d) 160

7. 54 ÷ ? = 6.

(a) 24   (b) 9   (c) 22   (d) 24

8. 5 + 10 - 15 + ? = 9

(a) 9   (b) 12   (c) 14   (d) 15

9. 6 - ? + 1 + 11 = 3.

(a) 15   (b) 16   (c) 17   (d) 18

10. $2 \times 7 \times 9$ = ?

(a) 97   (b) 126   (c) 121   (d) 111

11. $158 \div 2$ = ?

(a) 79   (b) 75   (c) 72   (d) 71

12. $28 \div ? = 7$.

(a) 4   (b)14   (c) 21   (d) 24

13. $3 \times 7 \times 2 \times 1$ = ?

(a) 28   (b) 41   (c) 42   (d) 49

14. -15 - 20 - 25 = ?

(a) 60   (b) 35   (c) -35   (d) -60

15. $2 \times 1 \times ? \times 1 = 2$.

(a) 1   (b) 2   (c) 3   (d) 4

16. 12 + 44 - 6 - 6 = ?

(a) 44   (b) 46   (c) 56   (d) 64

17. $(2 \times 12) \div (^{27}/_{9})$ = ?

(a) 4   (b) 8   (c) 12   (d) 1

18. $4^2 - 3^3$ = ?

(a) 11   (b) 10   (c) -11   (d) -10

19. $(24 - 5) \times 5$ = ?

(a) 85   (b) 95   (c) 105   (d) 115

20. 9 + 34 - 11 + 7 = ?

(a) 21   (b) 29   (c) 34   (d) 39

21. 27 - 56 + 5 + 11 = ?

(a) 13   (b) -11   (c) -13   (d) 11

22. ¼ × 60 = ?

(a) 14   (b) 30   (c) 21   (d) 15

23. 3 × 3 × 3 = ?

(a) 3^2 (b) 6   (c) 9   (d) 27

24. (2 × 7) × (3 + 1) = ?

(a) 42   (b) 45   (c) 56   (d) 59

25. (4 ÷ 8) × 4 = ?

(a) 0   (b) 2   (c) 4   (d) 8

26. 4 + (7 - 9) - 2 = ?

(a) 4   (b) 2   (c) 1   (d) 0

27. 27 + ¹⁶⁄₈ = ?

(a) 21   (b) 27   (c) 29   (d) 31

28. ¼ + ⅓ = ?

(a) ¾   (b) 4⅓   (c) ⁷⁄₁₂   (d) ⁴⁄₁₂

29. 14 - 14 - 14 + 7 = ?

(a) -7   (b) 7   (c) 14   (d) 14

30. (48 ÷ 12) × 12 = ?

(a) 24   (b) 48   (c) 60   (d) 74

31. 12 + 137 - 120 - 9 = ?

(a) 10   (b) 15   (c) 20   (d) 30

32. (10 × 100) - 90 + 5 = ?

(a) 915   (b) 900   (c) 845   (d) 815

33. 12 × 4 × 2 = ?

(a) 48   (b) 56   (c) 96   (d) 106

34. ⅓ ÷ ⅓ = ?

(a) 0   (b) 1   (c) 3   (d) 9

35. $(2 \times 2)^2$ = ?

(a) 0   (b) 4   (c) 8   (d) 16

36. (13 ÷ 7) × 7 = ?

(a) 11   (b) 13   (c) 7   (d) 17

37. 66 - 100 + 68 - 2 = ?

(a) 32   (b) 30   (c) 78   (d) 112

38. ⅗ × 80 = ?

(a) 12   (b) 24   (c) 36   (d) 48

39. (21 + 13) ÷ 34 = ?

(a) 1   (b) -1   (c) 0   (d) 2

40. ¼ × ¼ × ¼ = ?

(a) 4   (b) 1/64   (c) 1   (d) 1/16

41. 101 - 91 + 11 - 1 = ?

(a) 10   (b) 20   (c) 30   (d) 40

42. $9\frac{1}{4} + 12\frac{2}{4} = ?$

(a) $21\frac{3}{4}$ (b) $21\frac{1}{4}$ (c) $22\frac{3}{4}$ (d) $21\frac{3}{12}$

43. $5 \times 125 = ?$

(a) 525   (b) 575   (c) 600   (d) 625

44. $\frac{12}{6} - \frac{2}{3} = ?$

(a) $9\frac{1}{2}$ (b) $\frac{15}{12}$ (c) $1\frac{1}{12}$ (d) $\frac{2}{3}$

45. $3^3 \times 3 = ?$

(a) 9   (b) 27   (c) 56   (d) 81

46. $(45 \times 10) \div (12 - 2) = ?$

(a) 22.5   (b) 35   (c) 38   (d) 45

47. $(0.5 + 0.2) \times 2 = ?$

(a) 1.4   (b) 1.2   (c) 0.8   (d) 1.8

48. $1500 \times 0.21 = ?$

(a) 215   (b) 315   (c) 265   (d) 275

49. $34 - 64 + 10 - 2 = ?$

(a) -22   (b) 22   (c) 24   (d) -24

50. $\frac{121}{11} = ?$

(a) 11   (b) 1   (c) 1.1   (d) 12.1

Answers: 1. (c); **2.** (a); **3.** (d); **4.** (b); **5.** (c); **6.** (a); **7.** (b); **8.** (a); **9.** (a); **10.** (b); **11.** (a); **12.** (a); **13.** (c); **14.** (d); **15.** (a); **16.** (a); **17.** (b); **18.** (c); **19.** (b); **20.** (d); **21.** (c); **22.** (d); **23.** (d); **24.** (c); **25.** (b); **26.** (d); **27.** (c); **28.** (c); **29.** (a); **30.** (b); **31.** (c); **32.** (a); **33.** (c); **34.** (b); **35.** (d); **36.** (b); **37.** (a); **38.** (d); **39.** (a); **40.** (b); **41.** (b); **42.** (a); **43.** (d); **44.** (d); **45.** (d); **46.** (d); **47.** (a); **48.** (b); **49.** (a); **50.** (a).

Numerical Ability Power Test

In the following numerical ability power questions you need to identify the correct answer from the set of answer options provided. You can use a calculator if you want.

1. $t/4 = 7^{-2}$. **What is t?**

(a) 2   (b) 98   (c) 7^2 (d) 2^7

2. $(1 \times \frac{1}{2} \times 1)/2 = ?$

(a) -1   (b) 1   (c) 0   (d) 2

3. $\sqrt{5^2} =$

(a) 2.5   (b) 2^5 (c) 2   (d) 5

4. $(4q)/2 = 1$. **What is q?**

(a) 0   (b) ½   (c) 1   (d) 2

5. $a \times b = ?$

(a) ab   (b) a + b   (c) a   (d) b

6. $10\overline{)45634.5} = ?$

(a) 4563   (b) 45603   (c) 45634.5   (d) 4563.45

7. $2 \le n \ge 4$. **What is n?**

(a) 0   (b) 1   (c) 4   (d) 2

8. $3^y = 27$. **What is y?**

(a) 3   (b) 9   (c) 7   (d) 18

9. 5699874 - 7844 = ?

(a) 5692034   (b) 5692030   (c) 5692044   (d) 5692108

10. $2a + 2b = 2b + s$. *What is s?*

(a) 2a   (b) 2b   (c) -2a   (d) -2b

11. $55050 \div 25 = t$. *What is t?*

(a) 2022   (b) 2202   (c) 2220   (d) 2005

12. $(a + b) \times (x - y) = ax - ay + bx - m$. *What is m?*

(a) ab   (b) ba   (c) by   (d) ay

13. $^{32}/_{t} = ?$ *Where t = 2, what is ?*

(a) 8   (b)16   (c) 2t   (d) $^{16}/_{t}$

14. $-3(4) = p$. *What is p?*

(a) -12   (b) -6   (c) 6   (d) 12

15. $25.5 + \frac{3}{4} = ?$

(a) 18 ¼   (b) $^{22}/_{2}$ (c) 29.5   (d) 26 ¼

16. **20% of 50% of 100 = ?**

(a) 10   (b) 15   (c) 20   (d) 25

17. $2(x + y) - 3(x + y) = -1 (s)$. *What is s?*

(a) (xy)   (b) (-x - y)   (c) (x - y)   (d) (x + y)

18. $45 \times 4500 = ?$

(a) 22500   (b) 20250   (c) 220500   (d) 202500

19. $^{15}/_{p} = {}^{(3 \times t)}/_{p}$. *What is t?*

(a) 5   (b) 10   (c) 15   (d) 5p

20. $5q = \sqrt{625}$ *What is q?*

(a) 5   (b) 1   (c) 25   (d) 125

21. 6 (r × t) = ?

(a) 6r   (b) 6rt   (c) 6t   (d) rt

22. 660 × 210 = ?

(a) 13600   (b) 10633   (c) 138600   (d) 138606

23. $^{(5+y)}/_4$ = 8. *What is y?*

(a) 9   (b) 27   (c) 29   (d) 48

24. 4t + y = 5y. *What is t?*

(a) 2   (b) 4   (c) y   (d) 5

25. 5 < q. *What is q?*

(a) 2   (b) 3   (c) 4   (d) 6

26. $\sqrt{z}$ = 4   *What is z?*

(a) 4   (b) 8   (c) 12   (d) 16

27. 2(12y - 15y) = ?

(a) 6y   (b) -6y   (c) 12y   (d) -12y

28. 255 × 4050 = ?

(a) 1032705   (b) 11032750   (c) 103250   (d) 1032750

29 ¾ × 0.5 = ?

(a) 0.75   (b) ⅜   (c) 0.68   (d) ⅝

30. 75% of 4z = ?

(a) z   (b) 2z   (c) 3z   (d) 2z + 1

31. $4\overline{\smash{)}12}$ ÷ q = 1   *What is q?*

(a) 2   (b) 2q   (c) 3   (d) 4

32. $16 \times 1100 \times 10 = ?$

(a) 176000   (b) 176010   (c) 1760010   (d) 176006

33. $10\overline{)7892} = ?$

(a) 7890.2   (b) 789.2   (c) 78.92   (d) 7892

34. $4a = 2a + t$. *What is t?*

(a) a   (b) t   (c) 2a   (d) 3a

35. $2(t - y) = 2t$? $2y$. *What is '?'?*

(a) +   (b) ×   (c) -   (d) ÷

36. $6\overline{)n} = \dfrac{(2 \times n)}{y}$ *What is y?*

(a) 3   (b) 12   (c) 8   (d) 4

37. $\frac{2}{b} = \frac{6}{18}$. *What is b?*

(a) 2   (b) 6   (c) 14   (d) 18

38. $2(a + b) = 2a + t$. *What is t?*

(a) a   (b) 2b   (c) 2a   (d) a

39. Which of these answer options is greater?

(a) $\frac{17}{35}$ (b) 0.56   (c) $\frac{43}{19}$ (d) $\frac{19}{42}$

40. $22 \div m = 9 + m$. *What is m?*

(a) 2   (b) 0   (c) 11   (d) 9

Answers: 1. (b); **2.** (c); **3.** (d); **4.** (b); **5.** (a); **6.** (d); **7.** (c); **8.** (a); **9.** (b); **10.** (a); **11.** (b); **12.** (c); **13.** (b); **14.** (a); **15.** (d); **16.** (a); **17.** (d); **18.** (d); **19.** (a); **20.** (a); **21.** (b); **22.** (c); **23.** (b); **24.** (c); **25.** (d); **26.** (d); **27.** (b); **28.** (d); **29.** (b); **30.** (c); **31.** (c); **32.** (a); **33.** (b); **34.** (c); **35.** (c); **36.** (b); **37.** (b); **38.** (b); **39.** (c); **40.** (a).

Numerical Reasoning Speed Test

In the following numerical reasoning speed questions you need to identify the missing figure represented by the question mark from the set of answer options provided. You can use a calculator if you want.

1. **-5** **4** **-3** **2** **?**

(a) 0 (b) 1 (c) -1 (d) 2

2. **6** **7** **?** **8** **4**

(a) 2 (b) 3 (c) 4 (d) 5

3. **1:1** **2:8** **3:27** **4:?** **5:125**

(a) 64 (b) 59 (c) 34 (d) 95

4. **3** **0** **-3** **-9** **?**

(a) -10 (b) -12 (c) -15 (d) -18

5. **2** **8** **14** **?** **26**

(a) 18 (b) 19 (c) 20 (d) 24

6. **12** **6** **18** **9** **?**

(a) 21 (b) 24 (c) 27 (d) 29

7.

20	**10**	**5**
40	**20**	**?**
60	**30**	**15**

(a) 10 (b) 7 (c) 14 (d) 13

8. $\frac{1}{3}$ $\frac{3}{4}$ $\frac{4}{5}$ **?** $\frac{6}{7}$

(a) $\frac{2}{6}$ (b) $\frac{3}{6}$ (c) $\frac{5}{6}$ (d) $\frac{7}{6}$

9. 4   ?   8   8   16

(a) 4   (b) 5   (c) 6   (d) 7

10. $\frac{1}{3}$ is to $\frac{20}{4}$ as $\frac{1}{6}$ is to ?

(a) $\frac{48}{8}$ (b) $\frac{16}{12}$ (c) $\frac{18}{12}$ (d) $\frac{24}{8}$

11. 29   27   24   ?   15

(a) 21   (b) 20   (c) 19   (d) 18

12. 3   3   5   ?   19

(a) 13   (b) 15   (c) 16   (d) 17

13. 2   ?   4   6   4

(a) -1   (b) 0   (c) 1   (d) 2

14. 5   10   30   ?   180

(a) 60   (b) 50   (c) 48   (d) 42

15. 40% is to $\frac{2}{5}$ as ? is to $\frac{3}{8}$

(a) 20%   (b) 40%   (c) 25%   (d) 15%

16. H:8   10:J   ?   3:C   I:9

(a) 9:M   (b) 8:L   (c) 6:M   (d) 13:M

17. 1   3   4
     2   4   6
     3   7   ?

(a) 8   (b) 10   (c) 12   (d) 13

18. 18   27   36   ?   54

(a) 40   (b) 42   (c) 45   (d) 48

19. 11   7   5   3   ?

(a) 2   (b) 1   (c) 0   (d) -1

20. $\frac{5}{20}$ $\frac{1}{4}$ $\frac{4}{16}$ $\frac{3}{12}$ $\frac{6}{?}$

(a) 16   (b) 24   (c) 20   (d) 18

21. **8**   **6**   **12**   **?**   **20**

(a) 10   (b) 12   (c) 14   (d) 16

22. **15**   **17**   **20**   **?**   **29**

(a) 22   (b) 23   (c) 24   (d) 25

23. **13**   **15**   **30**   **?**   **64**

(a) 32   (b) 38   (c) 42   (d) 45

24. **3 is to $\frac{21}{7}$ as 4 is to $\frac{x}{9}$**

(a) 36   (b) 32   (c) 30   (d) 27

25. **?** $\frac{1}{27}$ $\frac{1}{9}$ $\frac{1}{3}$

(a) $\frac{1}{81}$ (b) $\frac{1}{72}$ (c) $\frac{1}{62}$ (d) $\frac{1}{56}$

26. **96**   **24**   **8**   **?**   **4**

(a) 7   (b) 4   (c) 6   (d) 5

27. **2.6 is to 1.3 as 4.5 is to ?**

(a) 2   (b) 2.75   (c) 2.5   (d) 2.25

28. **2**   **2**   **4**   **?**   **48**

(a) 10   (b) 11   (c) 12   (d) 13

29. **1**   **1**   **-2**   **?**   **24**

(a) 4   (b) -4   (c) -6   (d) 6

30. **$5\frac{1}{4}$ is to $\frac{42}{8}$ as $6\frac{5}{6}$ is to ?**

(a) $22\frac{2}{8}$ (b) $\frac{82}{12}$ (c) $\frac{64}{12}$ (d) $\frac{70}{12}$

31. $^{12}/_4$ $^{16}/_4$ $^{40}/_8$? $^{28}/_4$

(a) $^{12}/_9$ (b) 42   (c) $8^{7}/_{14}$ (d) $^{48}/_8$

32. 9 is to 99 as 1 is to ?

(a) 1   (b) 11   (c) -1   (d) 10

33. 5   25   1   1   ?

(a) -1   (b) 0   (c) 1   (d) 2

34. 15   30   ?   120   240

(a) 30   (b) 40   (c) 60   (d) 70

35. 0.2 $^{2}/_5$ 80%   ? $3\,^{1}/_5$

(a) 1.6   (b) 1.8   (c) 2   (d) $2\frac{1}{2}$

36. $^{40}/_8$ $^{28}/_7$ $^{27}/_9$ $^{14}/_7$?

(a) 0   (b) $^{3}/_4$ (c) 1   (d) 1.25

37. 4:3 is to 7 as ? is to 9

(a) 2:1   (b) 4:5   (c) 3:2   (d) 2:3

38. 9   16   178   ?   13259

(a) 1025   (b) 1000   (c) 10005   (d) 10025

39. 60   33   ?   27   36

(a) 50   (b) 56   (c) 61   (d) 66

40. 1 $^{2}/_7$ $^{3}/_9$ $^{4}/_{16}$ $^{5}/_{25}$

(a) 0   (b) 1   (c) 2   (d) 4

Answers: 1. (c); **2.** (d); **3.** (a); **4.** (b); **5.** (c); **6.** (c); **7.** (a); **8.** (c); **9.** (a); **10.** (a); **11.** (b); **12.** (b); **13.** (d); **14.** (a); **15.** (c); **16.** (d); **17.** (b); **18.** (c); **19.** (a); **20.** (b); **21.** (a); **22.** (c); **23.** (a); **24.** (a); **25.** (a); **26.** (b); **27.** (d); **28.** (c); **29.** (c); **30.** (b); **31.** (d); **32.** (b); **33.** (c); **34.** (c); **35.** (a); **36.** (c); **37.** (b); **38.** (a); **39.** (d); **40.** (d).

Numerical Reasoning Power Test

In this numerical reasoning power test, you need to read the following pieces of information and answer the questions you are asked. Identify the correct answer from the set of answer options you're given. You can use a calculator if you want.

1. The DVD Sale

You see this advert in a newspaper:

> ## SALE!
>
> All your favourite movies on DVD!
>
> Buy one DVD for the normal price of £10 and get one free when you present this voucher at the checkout.
>
> One voucher per customer. Offer finishes on Sunday.

(i) What is the normal price of a DVD?

(a) £10   (b) £8   (c) £15   (d) £5

(ii) If you bought a DVD on Saturday, how many DVDs would you receive free?

(a) 0   (b) 1   (c) 2   (d) 3

(iii) If you bought a DVD on Saturday, how many DVDs would you receive in total?

(a) 1   (b) 2   (c) 3   (d) 4

(iv) How much would four DVDs cost on Saturday?

(a) £5   (b) £10   (c) £20   (d) £30

(v) If you presented two vouchers at the checkout on Friday, how much would four DVDs cost?

(a) £5   (b) £10   (c) £20   (d) £30

(vi) How much would a DVD cost on Monday?

(a) £10   (b) £5   (c) £15   (d) £20

(vii) How much would a DVD cost on Sunday?

(a) £5   (b) £10   (c) £15   (d) £20

(viii) If you bought two DVDs on Sunday, how many DVDs would you receive free?

(a) 1   (b) 2   (c) 3   (d) 0

(ix) On which day would it be cheaper to buy four DVDs?

(a) Saturday (b) Sunday   (c) Monday   (d) All the same

(x) If you wanted three DVDs on Saturday, and shared the cost with a friend, how much would it cost you personally?

(a) £15   (b) £10   (c) £5   (d) £20

2. Calorie Burn

Look at the following information about the hourly rate at which a sample of 200 people of different ages burn calories during exercise.

Age (years)	Running	Cycling	Swimming
25	900	700	1,200
35	800	600	1,200
45	700	500	1,000

(i) How many 45-year olds were in the sample?

(a) 700   (b) 500   (c) 200   (d) Can't tell

(ii) What is the average calorie burn rate for cycling across all ages?

(a) 650   (b) 625   (c) 600   (d) 500

(iii) If a 35-year old went running for an hour, and then swam for an hour, how many calories would she burn?

(a) 2,000   (b) 1,200   (c) 800   (d) Can't tell

(iv) Which age group burns the least calories swimming?

(a) 45   (b) 35   (c) 25   (d) Can't tell

(v) Who burns the most calories – a 45-year old swimming or a 25-year old running?

(a) 45-year old   (b) 25-year old
(c) Both the same   (d) Can't tell

(vi) Which activity uses the most calories across all age groups?

(a) Running   (b) Cycling   (c) Swimming   (d) Can't tell

(vii) If someone burns 500 calories an hour during one form of exercise, how old is she?

(a) 45   (b) 35   (c) 25   (d) Can't tell

(viii) If someone burns 1200 calories an hour during one form of exercise, how old is she?

(a) 45   (b) 35   (c) 25   (d) Can't tell

(ix) If someone burns 700 calories an hour during one form of exercise, what is she doing?

(a) Running   (b) Cycling   (c) Swimming   (d) Can't tell

(x) Which activity uses the least calories across all age groups?

(a) Running   (b) Cycling   (c) Swimming   (d) Can't tell

3. The Journey to Work

You can travel to work using different modes of transport. The route you take changes depending upon the mode of transport you choose.

Mode of Transport	Speed (kilometres/hour)	Length of Route (kilometres)
Car	30	5
Bicycle	20	4
Bus	20	5
Walking	5	5

(i) Which is the fastest mode of transport?

(a) Car   (b) Walking   (c) Bicycle   (d) Bus

(ii) If you walked into work and were driven home by a colleague, how long would your two journeys take in total?

(a) 40 minutes   (b) 70 minutes
(c) 75 minutes   (d) 80 minutes

(iii) If you drove to and from work, how far would you travel in total?

(a) 8 kilometres   (b) 10 kilometres
(c) 12 kilometres   (d) 14 kilometres

(iv) How long would it take you to travel to work on foot?

(a) 30 minutes   (b) 60 minutes
(c) 75 minutes   (d) 90 minutes

(v) Which mode of transport would get you to work the quickest?

(a) Car   (b) Bicycle   (c) Walking   (d) Bus

(vi) If you waited 10 minutes for a bus to arrive, how long would the journey to work take?

(a) 15 minutes
(b) 20 minutes
(c) 25 minutes
(d) 30 minutes

(vii) How long would it take you to drive to work?

(a) 8 minutes
(b) 10 minutes
(c) 12 minutes
(d) 15 minutes

(viii) How long would it take you to cycle to work?

(a) 8 minutes
(b) 12 minutes
(c) 15 minutes
(d) 16 minutes

(ix) If you could cycle at 30 kilometres/hour, which mode of transport would get you to work the quickest?

(a) Walking   (b) Car   (c) Bicycle   (d) Bus

(x) If you took the bus to work and walked home at the end of the day, how much time would you spend travelling in total?

(a) 60 minutes
(b) 75 minutes
(c) 55 minutes
(d) 50 minutes

4. World Temperatures

The graph below shows the mean summer temperatures for four locations: A, B, C, and D. All locations are in the northern hemisphere.

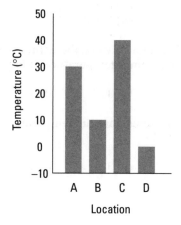

Mean temperatures decrease by 20% during the winter except in location D where it decreases by 10°C.

(i) What is the winter temperature in location A?

(a) 20°C   (b) 24°C   (c) 18°C   (d) 14°C

(ii) Which is warmer – location D in summer or location B in winter?

(a) Location D   (b) Location B

(iii) Which location has the smallest difference between summer and winter temperatures?

(a) Location A   (b) Location B
(c) Location C   (d) Location D

(iv) What is the winter temperature in location D?

(a) 0°C   (b) 10°C   (c) 5°C   (d) 10°C

(v) What is the difference between the summer and winter temperature in location C?

(a) 4°C   (b) 8°C   (c) 6°C   (d) 10°C

(vi) Which location has the largest difference between summer and winter temperatures?

(a) Location A   (b) Location B
(c) Location C   (d) Location D

(vii) What is the difference between the winter temperature in location C and the summer temperature in location D?

(a) 22°C   (b) 24°C   (c) 30°C   (d) 32°C

(viii) In how many locations does the temperature fall below 30°C during the winter?

(a) 1   (b) 2   (c) 3   (d) 4

(ix) In how many locations is the temperature between 15°C and 32°C during the winter?

(a) 1   (b) 2   (c) 3   (d) 4

(x) The temperature in location D never rises above freezing.

(a) True   (b) False   (c) Can't tell

5. The Sales Team

Here is a set of annual sales figures. Commission is paid on all income above target sales. Note that 'k' is thousand, so £50k means the same as £50,000.

Name	Basic Salary	Commission	Target Sales	Actual Sales
Sally	£15,000	10%	£100k	£50k
John	£12,000	20%	£100k	£100k
Mina	£20,000	20%	£120k	£150k
Alice	£18,000	10%	£110k	£140k
Brian	£22,000	10%	£150k	£120k

(i) How many people will receive no bonus this year?

(a) 1   (b) 2   (c) 3   (d) 4

(ii) Who earns the most money?

(a) Mina   (b) Alice   (c) Brian   (d) John

(iii) What would Alice's sales need to be in order for her to earn a bonus of £5,000?

(a) £100k   (b) £120k   (c) £140k   (d) £160k

(iv) Who is the worst performing seller?

(a) John   (b) Sally   (c) Mina   (d) Brian

(v) Who will earn the least?

(a) John   (b) Sally   (c) Alice   (d) Brian

(vi) Who has the largest gap between target sales and actual sales?

(a) Sally   (b) Mina   (c) Alice   (d) Brian

(vii) What will Alice's bonus be?

(a) £3,500   (b) £3,000   (c) £4,000   (d) £2,500

(viii) What will Mina's total income be?

(a) £13,100   (b) £25,400   (c) £26,000   (d) £32,000

(ix) What is the difference in income between the best and worst earners in the team?

(a) £12,000   (b) £14,000   (c) £15,000   (d) £16,000

(x) Who has the best commission-to-target sales ratio?

(a) Sally   (b) Mina   (c) John   (d) Brian

6. River Levels

This table describes the effect of rainfall on the increase in height above normal flow level, and the water flow rate of a river. The normal river level is 12 inches. Water drainage from adjoining fields accounts for the increase in river levels when there has been zero rainfall.

Rainfall (inches/hour)	Increase in River Height (inches)	Flow Rate (litres³/sec)
0	2	100
1	4	200
2	4	300
3	6	400

(i) What is the flow rate in litres³/sec most likely to be for four inches of rainfall per hour?

(a) 400   (b) 500   (c) 600   (d) 700

(ii) For one inch of rainfall, what will the litres³ flow rate be per minute?

(a) 4,000   (b) 5,500   (c) 5,700   (d) 12,000

(iii) What is the average increase in river height?

(a) 1 inch   (b) 2 inches   (c) 3 inches   (d) 4 inches

(iv) If the flow rate per minute is 24,000 litres, how many inches of rain have fallen?

(a) 0   (b) 1   (c) 2   (d) 3

(v) What is the average flow rate per second in litres³?

(a) 100   (b) 150   (c) 250   (d) 300

(vi) If the river height has increased by four inches, and the flow rate is 18,000 litres per minute, how many inches of rainfall per hour have fallen?

(a) 0   (b) 1   (c) 2   (d) 3

(vii) If rainfall is one inch per hour, how much rain will fall in 30 minutes?

(a) ½ inch   (b) 1 inch   (c) 1½ inches   (d) 2 inches

(viii) How much more flow per second in litres³ is there when the river increases from two to six inches?

(a) 100   (b) 200   (c) 300   (d) 400

(ix) How many inches of rainfall per hour would cause the river to flow fastest?

(a) 0   (b) 1   (c) 2   (d) 3

(x) By how much will the river level increase after one inch of rain?

(a) 1   (b) 2   (c) 3   (d) 4

7. Production Error Rate

A machine sprays pallets of timber with preservative as they emerge from a production line. Quality control always reveals at least a few errors in the spraying process. When this occurs, the pallets of timber must be returned to the start of the production line to be sprayed again.

Pallets (per hour)	Errors (% of pallets)	Litres of Preservative Used (per hour)
500	4	50
800	8	80
1,000	8	100
1,200	10	120
1,500	20	150

(i) How many litres of preservative would be used if the rate of production increased to 2,000 pallets per hour?

(a) 100   (b) 200   (c) 300   (d) 400

(ii) If 250 pallets of timber were sprayed, how many litres of preservative would be used?

(a) 15   (b) 25   (c) 30   (d) 35

(iii) At a 10% error rate how many error-free pallets are produced?

(a) 1,088   (b) 1,188   (c) 1,018   (d) 1,080

(iv) If 800 pallets per hour are being sprayed, how many litres of preservative are used over a three-hour period?

(a) 240   (b) 140   (c) 200   (d) 440

(v) If 500 pallets are sprayed per hour for one hour, and then 1,500 pallets are sprayed per hour for one hour, how many litres of preservative are used?

(a) 50   (b) 100   (c) 200   (d) 300

(vi) If 1,500 pallets are sprayed per hour, how many will have errors?

(a) 200   (b) 300   (c) 400   (d) 500

(vii) If the spraying machine indicates it has used 240 litres of preservative, how many pallets have been sprayed?

(a) 1,200   (b) 2,400   (c) 2,800   (d) 3,200

(viii) If the machine sprays pallets at a rate of 1,200 per hour for one hour, and then suffers a 10% slow down for two hours, and then resumes spraying at a rate of 800 pallets per hour for one hour, how many pallets will be sprayed?

(a) 2,140   (b) 2,260   (c) 4,160   (d) 4,610

(ix) The spraying machine has become clogged and can only spray preservative at 40% of its previous rate. If it now sprays 600 pallets per hour, what must its previous rate of production have been?

(a) 500   (b) 1,500   (c) 2,000   (d) 2,500

(x) What is the average number of litres of preservative used per hour?

(a) 25   (b) 50   (c) 75   (d) 100

8. Staff Holidays

Staff are entitled to five weeks paid holiday per year. The exceptions are when an employee has been with the company less than one year (in which case she's entitled to only four weeks paid holiday), or when an employee has been with the company for more than ten years (in which case she's entitled to seven weeks paid holiday). All staff may get an additional one-week of discretionary paid holiday as a bonus.

(i) What is the maximum number of weeks paid holiday an employee can possibly have?

(a) 8   (b) 6   (c) 5   (d) 4

(ii) What is the most holiday an employee can possibly have?

(a) 4 weeks   (b) 5 weeks   (c) 8 weeks   (d) 9 weeks

(iii) After nine years of service, how much additional discretionary paid holiday can an employee have?

(a) 1 week   (b) 2 weeks   (c) 3 weeks   (d) 4 weeks

(iv) If an employee is entitled to 4 weeks holiday, how long has she been with the company?

(a) Less than 1 year   (b) 1 year   (c) 9 years   (d) 10 years

(v) What is the minimum amount of holiday an employee can possibly have?

(a) 4 weeks   (b) 5 weeks   (c) 6 weeks   (d) 7 weeks

(vi) If an employee has 7 weeks holiday, how long has she been with the company?

(a) 5 years   (b) 8 years   (c) 9 years   (d) More than 10 years

(vii) In January, an employee celebrates being with the company for 10 years. To how much holiday is she entitled to in total?

(a) 2 weeks   (b) 4 weeks   (c) 8 weeks   (d) 9 weeks

(viii) If an employee has 6 weeks holiday, how many years has she been with the company?

(a) Less than 1   (b) 2 to 10   (c) 11   (d) 12

(ix) An employee of 5 years doesn't get any discretionary holiday this year. Can an employee of less than 1 year get more holiday than her?

(a) Yes   (b) No   (c) Can't tell

(x) What is the maximum number of weeks holiday an employee can possibly have over the first 4 years with the company?

(a) 12   (b) 16   (c) 23   (d) 24

9. Sunrise and Sunset

The times of sunrise and sunset at a particular location in the UK are detailed in this table. In the UK, British Summer Time (BST) runs from March to October and one hour is added to these times during these months.

Month	Sunrise	Sunset
January	8.15	5.15
April	6.30	7.00
July	5.30	9.30
October	6.45	6.45

(i) What time is sunrise in April?

(a) 5.30   (b) 7.30   (c) 7.45   (d) 8.15

(ii) How many hours of daylight are there in January?

(a) 7   (b) 8   (c) 9   (d) 10

(iii) How many hours of darkness are there in October?

(a) 8   (b) 10   (c) 11   (d) 12

(iv) When is the latest sunset?

(a) January   (b) April   (c) July   (d) October

(v) What time is sunset in July?

(a) 9.45   (b) 10.30   (c) 10.45   (d) 11.30

(vi) When are there most hours of darkness?

(a) January   (b) April   (c) July   (d) October

(vii) What time does the sun rise in October?

(a) 6.45   (b) 7.45   (c) 8.00   (d) 8.15

(viii) If BST ran from May to November then the sun would rise earlier in July than it would in April.

(a) True   (b) False   (c) Both the same   (d) Can't tell

(ix) If a BST adjustment wasn't applied, when would the earliest sunset be?

(a) 4.15   (b) 5.15   (c) 6.15   (d) 7.15

(x) During BST, by how much does the length of day increase?

(a) 0 hours   (b) 1 hour   (c) 2 hours   (d) 3 hours

10. Quarterly Sales Figures

Quarter	DVD Sales	Video Sales	CD Sales	Book Sales
Q1	15,000	8,000	11,000	18,000
Q2	25,000	6,500	10,000	20,000
Q3	21,000	6,500	12,000	22,000
Q4	35,000	5,500	12,000	20,000

Average DVD cost: £10. Average video cost: £15. Average CD cost: £14. Average book cost: £10. The year runs from 1 April to 31 March.

(i) Most DVDs were sold in the first half of the year.

(a) True   (b) False   (c) Can't tell

(ii) The highest book sales were over the Christmas period.

(a) True   (b) False   (c) Can't tell

(iii) Sales of which product generated most income in Q1?

(a) DVDs   (b) Videos   (c) CDs   (d) Books

(iv) What was the lowest selling product in Q2?

(a) DVDs   (b) Videos   (c) CDs   (d) Books

(v) Videos and books outsold DVDs and CDs in Q3.

(a) True   (b) False   (c) Can't tell

(vi) When were the poorest video sales?

(a) Q1   (b) Q2   (c) Q3   (d) Q4

(vii) What was the annual income generated by DVD sales?

(a) £96,000   (b) £960,000   (c) £9.9 million

(viii) What is likely to happen to video sales in Q1 next year?

(a) Increase   (b) Can't tell   (c) Decrease

(ix) When does the New Year fall?

(a) Q1   (b) Q2   (c) Q3   (d) Q4

(x) Which product sold best across Q2 to Q4 inclusive?

(a) DVDs   (b) Videos   (c) CDs   (d) Books

11. Population Age Ranges

Three different random samples of 1,000 people were surveyed over three successive years.

Age Range	Percentage of the Population Year 1	Percentage of the Population Year 2	Percentage of the Population Year 3
0-19	20	15	10
20-39	20	25	35
40-59	30	25	25
60-79	25	20	25

(i) What percentage of the sample is older than 79 in year one?

(a) 5%   (b) 15%   (c) 20%   (d) 25%

(ii) In year one, more people are in the age range 40 59 than in age range 20 – 39 in year three.

(a) True   (b) False   (c) Can't tell

(iii) What percentage of people are older than 79 in year two?

(a) 5%   (b) 15%   (c) 20%   (d) 25%

(iv) How many people are aged between 20 and 59 in year two?

(a) 200   (b) 300   (c) 400   (d) 500

(v) In which year are more people in the age range 0 – 19 than there are people older than 79?

(a) 1   (b) 2   (c) 3   (d) None of them

(vi) Which year has the highest proportion of people under 40?

(a) 1   (b) 2   (c) 3   (d) None of them

(vii) What will happen to the size of the 0 – 19 age group?

(a) Increase   (b) Decrease (c) Stay the same

(viii) How many people were there aged 40 – 59 in year one?

(a) 200   (b) 220   (c) 260   (d) 300

(ix) How many fewer people aged 20 – 39 were there in year one compared to year three?

(a) 100   (b) 125   (c) 150   (d) 175

(x) Compare the number people aged over 79 in year three to year two. Are there:

(a) 50 fewer   (b) 100 fewer   (c) 100 more   (d) 50 more

12. The Exam

In a 3-hour exam, candidates can choose to complete one of the following:

- ✔ Option 1: Three long questions
- ✔ Option 2: One long question and six short questions
- ✔ Option 3: Two long questions and three short questions
- ✔ Option 4: Nine short questions

During the exam, you're allowed a maximum of an hour to complete each long question. The course being examined contains 12 subjects and it takes a day to revise for each.

(i) What proportion of subjects are covered by option 4?

(a) 25%   (b) 50%   (c) 75%   (d) 100%

(ii) If you only revised half of the topics, which option gives you the best chance of being able to answer all the questions you chose?

(a) Option 1 (b) Option 2   (c) Option 3   (d) Option 4

(iii) If you chose option 3, but were only able to answer one long question and two short questions, how much time would it take?

(a) 60 minutes   (b) 100 minutes   (c) 110 minutes   (d) 120 minutes

(iv) If you chose option 2 and spent 2 hours 40 minutes answering questions, how many questions would be left unanswered?

(a) 1 short   (b) 2 short   (c) 2 short and 1 long   (d) 2 long

(v) How long would it take to revise for every topic?

(a) 6 days   (b) 8 days   (c) 10 days   (d) 12 days

(vi) If you chose option 3 and decided to answer one long question, followed by one short question, how much time would you then have remaining in the exam?

(a) 60 minutes   (b) 100 minutes   (c) 110 minutes   (d) 120 minutes

(vii) If you arrived half an hour late for the exam, which option would allow you to complete the most questions?

(a) Option 1   (b) Option 2   (c) Option 3   (d) Option 4

(viii) Which option allows you to complete the fewest questions?

(a) Option 1   (b) Option 2   (c) Option 3   (d) Option 4

(ix) If you revised for seven days which option should you avoid?

(a) Option 1   (b) Option 2   (c) Option 3   (d) Option 4

(x) What is the minimum number of days you need to revise to give yourself a chance of answering all the questions in option 3?

(a) 2 days   (b) 3 days   (c) 4 days   (d) 5 days

13. *Software Development*

A 'compiler' is a tool used to build lines of code into finished software. One particular software developer can choose from three different compilers to build their software.

Compiler	Site Licence Cost p/a	Pro- rata Build Cost per 1,000 Lines of Code	Build Time per 1,000 Lines of Code
A	£8,000	£5	20 minutes
B	£5,000	£10	20 minutes
C	£10,000	£15	5 minutes

Note: The site licence fee reduces by 50% in the second year.

(i) What is the cost of a two-year site licence for compiler C?

(a) £10,000   (b) £15,000   (c) £16,000   (d) £18,000

(ii) Excluding the site licence, what does it cost to build 5,500 lines of code using compiler B?

(a) £55   (b) £80   (c) £85   (d) £90

(iii) Including the first year site licence, how much does it cost to compile 1,100 lines of code using compiler A?

(a) £12,000   (b) £8,005.50   (c) £14,500   (d) £15,000

(iv) Compiler B is used four times in the first two years to build 1,500 lines of code each time. What is the total cost?

(a) £1,060   (b) £ 1,560   (c) £4,060   (d) £7,650

(v) Excluding the site licence, which compiler would build 1,000 lines of code for the least cost?

(a) Compiler A   (b) Compiler B   (c) Compiler C

(vi) Which compiler would build 1,780 lines of code the quickest?

(a) Compiler A   (b) Compiler B   (c) Compiler C

(vii) Including the site licence, which compiler would build 1,000 lines of code for the least cost?

(a) Compiler A   (b) Compiler B   (c) Compiler C

(viii) If cost was not a consideration, which compiler would be the quickest?

(a) Compiler A   (b) Compiler B   (c) Compiler C

(ix) If you had £6,000 to spend over one year and had 1,500 lines of code to build, which compiler(s) would you use?

(a) Compiler A   (b) Compiler B   (c) Compiler C

(x) Which compiler provides the lowest cost per minute per line of code built?

(a) Compiler A   (b) Compiler B   (c) Compiler C

14. The Body Repair Shop

A car repair shop makes the following charges:

Nature of Work	Charge
Bare metal respray	£1,800
Top coat respray	£450
Body repair work	£50 per hour for first 10 hours, and then £40 per hour. Panels charged per replacement panel used.
Metallic paint	Add 20% to respray cost
Overnight storage (a day being 8 hours)	£40

(i) How much would it cost to carry out a bare metal respray in red metallic paint?

(a) £1,266   (b) £1,866   (c) £2,060   (d) £2,160

(ii) If you left a vehicle overnight for a top-coat respray to be completed the next day, how much would it cost you in total?

(a) £410   (b) £420   (c) £490   (d) £510

(iii) What is the cost per hour for the first hour of panel repair work?

(a) £0   (b) £40   (c) £50   (d) £60

(iv) How much extra is a metallic paint respray?

(a) £20%   (b) 25%£   (c) 35%£   (d) £40%

(v) How much would you pay in overnight storage fees if the work took 3 days?

(a) £80   (b) £120   (c) £160   (d) £200

(vi) How much would it cost for the replacement of one panel (price £70), which took one day to do, plus another day to carry out a top-coat respray?

(a) £960   (b) £1,020   (c) £1,200   (d) £1,400

(vii) You have your car bare-metal sprayed red, change your mind and have the top-coat resprayed metallic blue. Your car requires storage overnight. How much does it cost in total?

(a) £2,080   (b) £2,380   (c) £4,200   (d) £4,900

(viii) How much more expensive is a metallic paint bare metal respray than a non-metallic paint bare metal respray?

(a) £360   (b) £ 380   (c) £420   (d) £430

(ix) If the existing panels can be repaired, how much would 20 hours of panel work cost?

(a) £700   (b) £900   (c) £1,000   (d) £1,100

(x) Doing 32 hours of panel work is cheaper than carrying out a bare metal metallic respray.

(a) True   (b) False   (c) Both the same   (d) Can't tell

15. Childcare Rates

A day nursery provides childcare according to the following scale. If two siblings are registered at the nursery then the fees for the youngest child attract a 10% discount.

Age	½ Day Rate	Full Day Rate	Full Week
0 – 17 months	£25	£45	£200
18 months – 23 months	£25	£40	£180
2 – 3 years	£20	£35	£175
4 years plus	£20	£30	£140

(i) How much does it cost to keep two siblings, aged 2 and 3, in the nursery for one day?

(a) £70   (b) £66.50   (c) £75   (d) £77

(ii) How much cheaper per week does it become for childcare when a child reaches her 4th birthday?

(a) £25   (b) £30   (c) £35   (d) £40

(iii) How much would the fees be for two 1-year old siblings per week?

(a) £260   (b) £280   (c) £320   (d) £380

(iv) If it costs £161 for two siblings to attend for two full days a week, and one of them is 9 months old, how old must her sibling be?

(a) 12 months (b) 18 – 23 months (c) 2 years   (d) 3 years

(v) How much more expensive is it to keep a 2-year old in nursery for two half days than it is for one full day?

(a) £5   (b) £10   (c) £15   (d) £20

(vi) Which is cheaper – having a 3-year old in nursery all week, or a 6-month old in nursery for four days?

(a) 6-month old   (b) 3-year old
(c) Both the same   (d) Can't tell

(vii) How much does it cost to keep a 1-year old in nursery for two days and his 4-year-old sister in nursery for a week?

(a) £122   (b) £221   (c) £225   (d) £261

(viii) It is cheaper for a 3-year old to attend nursery for three full days and two half days than to attend for a full week.

(a) True   (b) False   (c) Can't tell

(ix) How much would it cost for a 2-year old to attend for two full days one week, three full days the second week, and two half days the third week?

(a) £155   (b) £165   (c) £215   (d) £225

(x) If it costs £105 for a child to attend nursery for two and a half days, how old must she be?

(a) 18 – 23 months   (b) 1 year
(c) 2 years   (d) 3 years

Answers to *Question 1. The DVD Sale:* (i) a; **(ii)** b; **(iii)** b; **(iv)** d; **(v)** d; **(vi)** a; **(vii)** b; **(viii)** a; **(ix)** d; **(x)** b.

Answers to *Question 2. Calorie Burn:* (i) d; **(ii)** c; **(iii)** a; **(iv)** a; **(v)** a; **(vi)** c; **(vii)** a; **(viii)** d; **(ix)** d; **(x)** b.

Answers to *Question 3. The Journey to Work:* (i) a; **(ii)** b; **(iii)** b; **(iv)** b; **(v)** a; **(vi)** c; **(vii)** b; **(viii)** b; **(ix)** c; **(x)** b.

Answers to *Question 4. World Temperatures:* (i) b; **(ii)** b; **(iii)** b; **(iv)** b; **(v)** b; **(vi)** d; **(vii)** d; **(viii)** c; **(ix)** b; **(x)** a.

Answers to *Question 5. The Sales Team:* (i) c; **(ii)** a; **(iii)** d; **(iv)** b; **(v)** a; **(vi)** a; **(vii)** b; **(viii)** c; **(ix)** b; **(x)** c.

Answers to *Question 6. River Levels:* (i) b; **(ii)** d; **(iii)** d; **(iv)** d; **(v)** c; **(vi)** c; **(vii)** a; **(viii)** c; **(ix)** c; **(x)** d.

Answers to *Question 7. Production Error Rate:* (i) b; **(ii)** b; **(iii)** d; **(iv)** a; **(v)** c; **(vi)** b; **(vii)** b; **(viii)** c; **(ix)** b; **(x)** b.

Answers to *Question 8. Staff Holidays:* (i) a; **(ii)** c; **(iii)** a; **(iv)** a; **(v)** a; **(vi)** d; **(vii)** c; **(viii)** b; **(ix)** b; **(x)** c.

Answers to *Question 9. Sunrise and Sunset:* (i) b; **(ii)** c; **(iii)** d; **(iv)** c; **(v)** b; **(vi)** a; **(vii)** b; **(viii)** b; **(ix)** b; **(x)** a.

Answers to *Question 10. Quarterly Sales Figures:* (i) b; **(ii)** a; **(iii)** d; **(iv)** b; **(v)** b; **(vi)** d; **(vii)** a; **(viii)** b; **(ix)** d; **(x)** a.

Answers to *Question 11. Population Age Ranges:* (i) a; **(ii)** b; **(iii)** b; **(iv)** d; **(v)** d; **(vi)** c; **(vii)** b; **(viii)** d; **(ix)** c; **(x)** b.

Answers to *Question 12. The Exam:* (i) c; **(ii)** a; **(iii)** b; **(iv)** a; **(v)** d; **(vi)** b; **(vii)** d; **(viii)** a; **(ix)** d; **(x)** d.

Answers to *Question 13. Software Development:* (i) b; **(ii)** a; **(iii)** b; **(iv)** d; **(v)** a; **(vi)** c; **(vii)** c; **(viii)** c; **(ix)** b; **(x)** a.

Answers to *Question 14. The Body Repair Shop:* (i) d; **(ii)** c; **(iii)** c; **(iv)** a; **(v)** a; **(vi)** a; **(vii)** b; **(viii)** a; **(ix)** b; **(x)** a.

Answers to *Question 15. Childcare Rates:* (i) b; (ii) c; (iii) d; (iv) b; (v) a; (vi) b; (vii) b; (viii) a; (ix) c; (x) a.

Chapter 12

Abstract Ability Sample Tests

* *

In This Chapter

▶ Checking out your creativity

▶ Scrutinising your strategic abilities

▶ Finding the answers

* *

*H*ere we delve into abstract ability tests and include tests of creativity and strategic reasoning ability. Employers like these tests because they are good at demonstrating your ability to problem-solve when you have little prior experience to benefit from. You can just dip in and have a quick look, or if you want to push yourself, try the whole test using the time limits shown in Table 12–1.

Table 12–1   Abstract Ability Sample Test Time Limits

Type of Test	Time Limit
Creativity Speed Test	**25 minutes**
Creativity Power Tests	
Odd One Out	25 minutes
Relationships	25 minutes
Strategic Thinking Test	**Untimed**

You can find the correct answers at the end of each test.

These tests are set at an average level of difficulty – one that most people find to be challenging, but achievable – and not with the correct answers beyond the reach of everyone but the Einsteins among us! This means that you're most likely to see the answer I intend you to see. However, in the creativity tests particularly, other more complex answers that you can spot may be present. If you're feeling really on the ball, you may well find alternative answers that are also correct. If so, well done! If not, try to look for alternative answers anyway; it's an excellent way to practice.

Creativity Speed Test

This test is a 'next in sequence' test. You have to identify the theme linking the first set of patterns, and then choose from the patterns that follow the one that you think should be next in the sequence. Circle the pattern that you think is the correct answer.

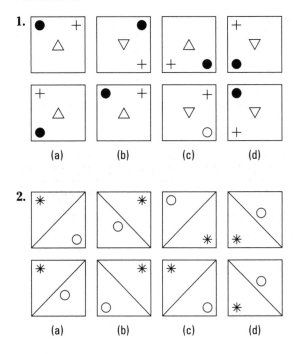

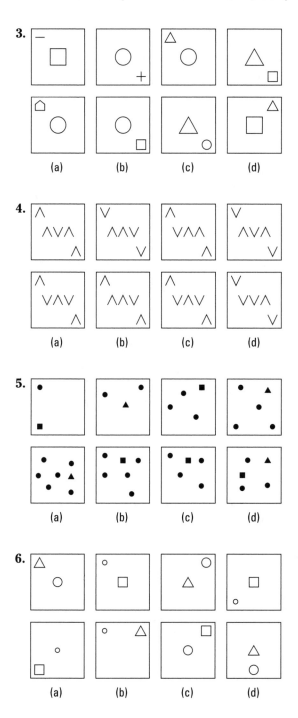

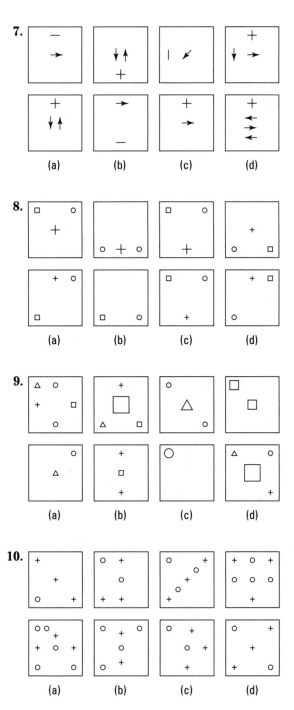

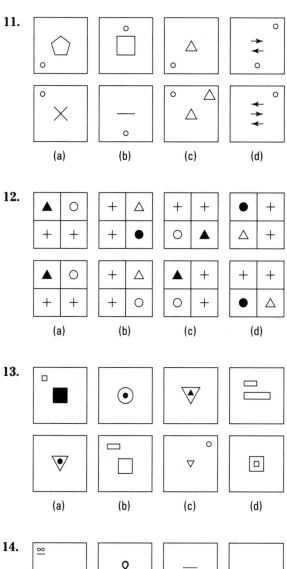

11.

(a)   (b)   (c)   (d)

12.

(a)   (b)   (c)   (d)

13.

(a)   (b)   (c)   (d)

14.

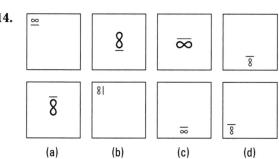

(a)   (b)   (c)   (d)

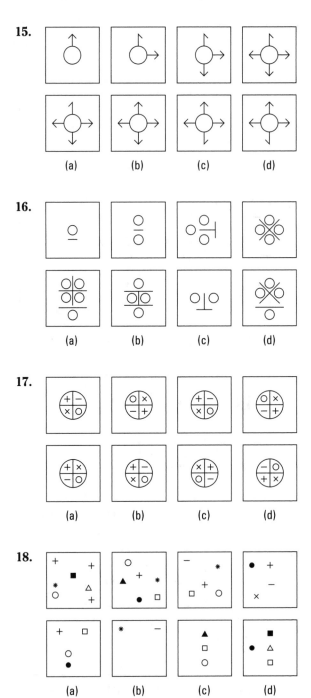

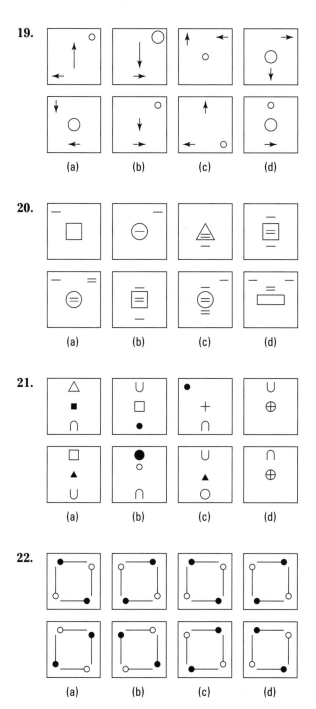

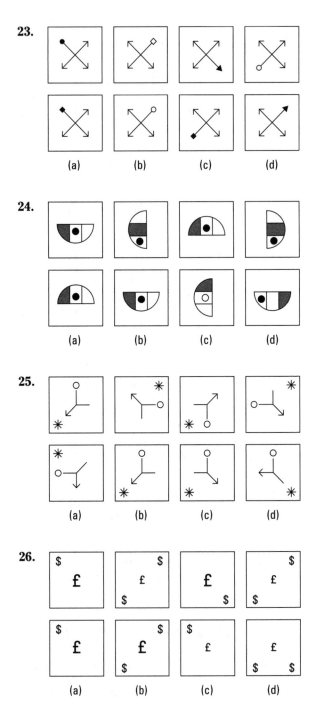

23.

(a) (b) (c) (d)

24.

(a) (b) (c) (d)

25.

(a) (b) (c) (d)

26.

(a) (b) (c) (d)

27.

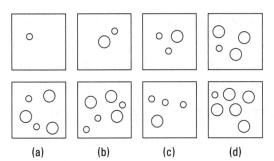

(a)   (b)   (c)   (d)

28.

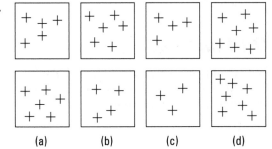

(a)   (b)   (c)   (d)

29.

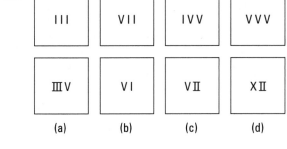

(a)   (b)   (c)   (d)

30.

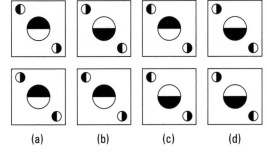

(a)   (b)   (c)   (d)

Answers: 1. (b); **2.** (c); **3.** (a); **4.** (b); **5.** (b); **6.** (c); **7.** (b); **8.** (c); **9.** (c); **10.** (a); **11.** (b); **12.** (a); **13.** (d); **14.** (c); **15.** (b); **16.** (a); **17.** (b); **18.** (c); **19.** (c); **20.** (a); **21.** (b); **22.** (d); **23.** (a); **24.** (b); **25.** (b); **26.** (a); **27.** (a); **28.** (c); **29.** (a); **30.** (b).

Creativity Power Tests

These creativity power tests are a little more difficult than the speed tests. Remember to think creatively – of things other than what's immediately obvious to you – as you tackle the questions.

Odd one out

In this 'odd one out' test you have to identify which pattern is the odd one out from a series of five. Circle the pattern that you think is the odd one out.

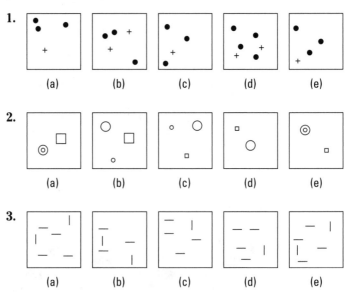

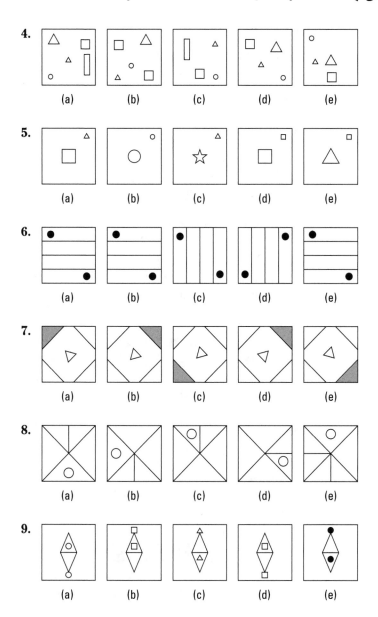

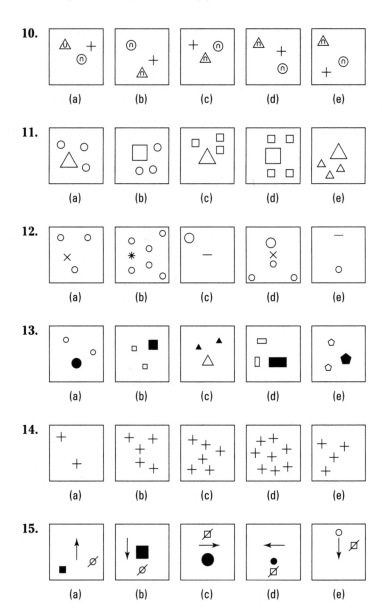

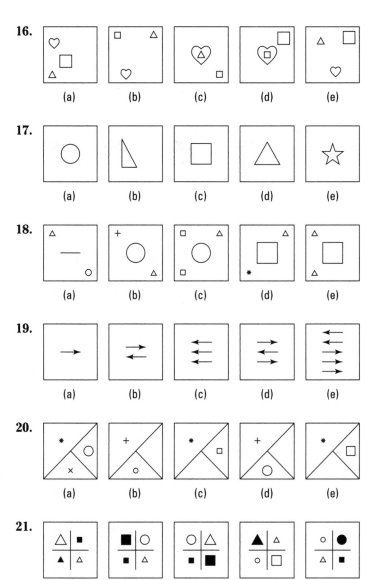

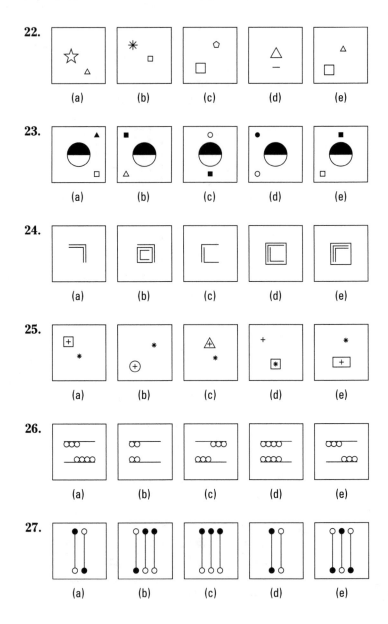

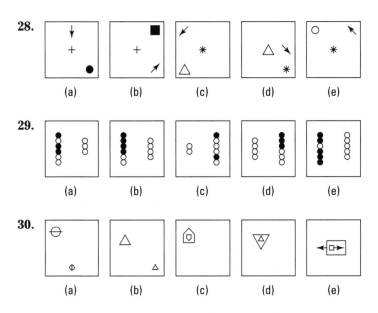

Answers: 1. (d); **2.** (d); **3.** (b); **4.** (c); **5.** (b); **6.** (c); **7.** (b); **8.** (e); **9.** (b); **10.** (a); **11.** (b); **12.** (a); **13.** (c); **14.** (b); **15.** (e); **16.** (d); **17.** (b); **18.** (c); **19.** (b); **20.** (a); **21.** (d); **22.** (c); **23.** (c); **24.** (b); **25.** (d); **26.** (a); **27.** (d); **28.** (a); **29.** (d); **30.** (b).

Relationships

In this relationships test you have to identify how the first pair of objects relate to each other, and then apply that rule to the third object and choose which of the objects that follow completes the second pair. Circle your chosen answer.

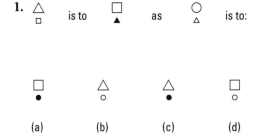

2.

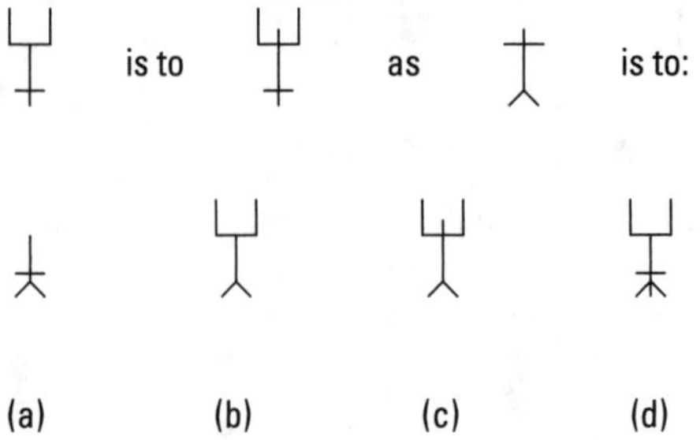
is to
as
is to:
(a)
(b)
(c)
(d)

3.

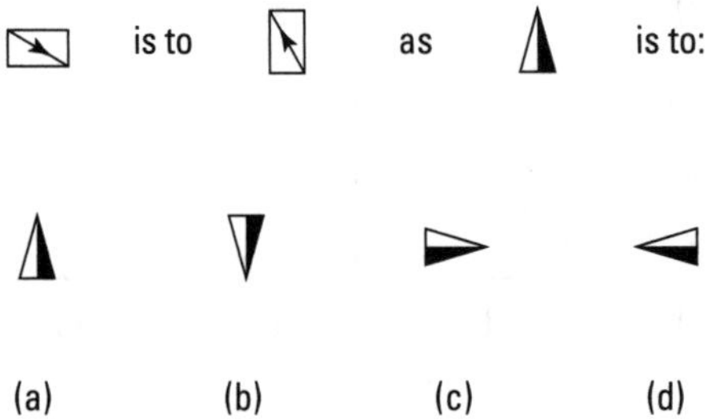
is to
as
is to:
(a)
(b)
(c)
(d)

4.

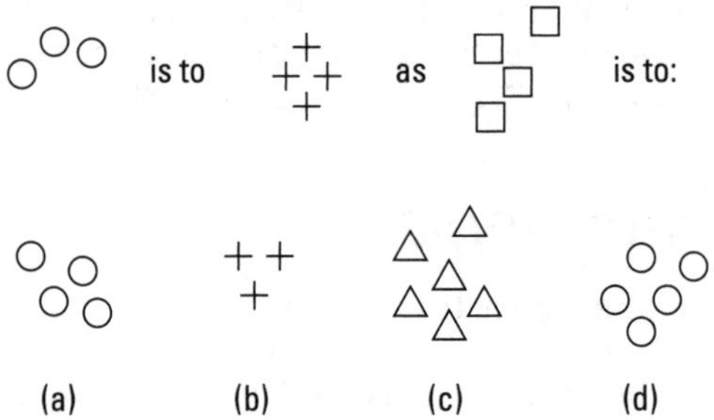
is to
as
is to:
(a)
(b)
(c)
(d)

5.

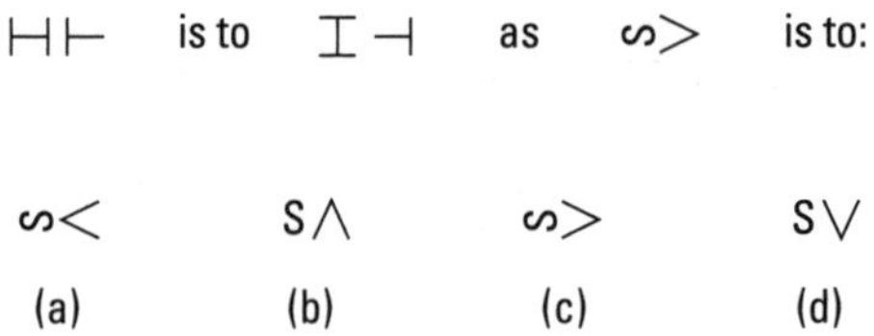
is to
as
is to:
(a)
(b)
(c)
(d)

6. is to as is to:

    (a)   (b)   (c)   (d)

7. is to as is to:

    (a)   (b)   (c)   (d)

8. is to as is to:

    (a)   (b)   (c)   (d)

9. is to as is to:

    (a)   (b)   (c)   (d)

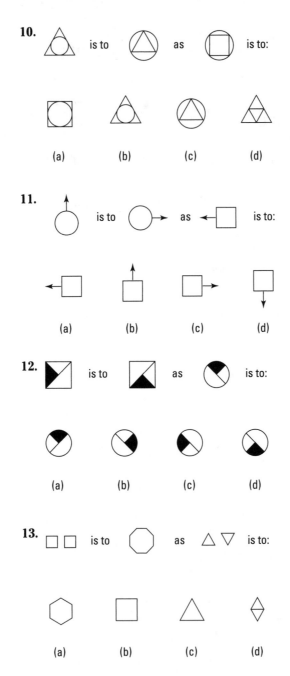

10. △ is to ⊕ as ▢ is to:

(a) (b) (c) (d)

11. is to as is to:

(a) (b) (c) (d)

12. is to as is to:

(a) (b) (c) (d)

13. is to as is to:

(a) (b) (c) (d)

14.

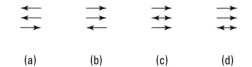

(a) (b) (c) (d)

15.

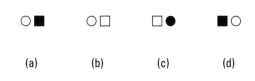

(a) (b) (c) (d)

16.

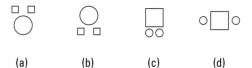

(a) (b) (c) (d)

17.

(a) (b) (c) (d)

18.

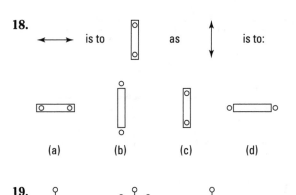

(a)   (b)   (c)   (d)

19.

(a)   (b)   (c)   (d)

20.

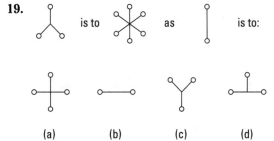

(a)   (b)   (c)   (d)

21.

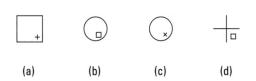

(a)   (b)   (c)   (d)

22.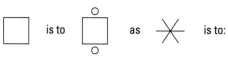

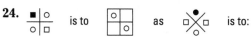

(a)　　　　(b)　　　　(c)　　　　(d)

23. 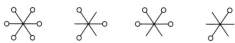 is to:

(a)　　　　(b)　　　　(c)　　　　(d)

24. is to as is to:

(a)　　　　(b)　　　　(c)　　　　(d)

25.

(a)　　　　(b)　　　　(c)　　　　(d)

26.

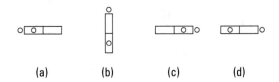

(a)   (b)   (c)   (d)

27.

is to   as   is to:

(a)   (b)   (c)   (d)

28.

is to   as   is to:

(a)   (b)   (c)   (d)

29.

is to   as   is to:

(a)   (b)   (c)   (d)

30.

△	□
✳	+

is to

✳	△
+	□

as

A	B
8	2

is to:

8	A
2	B

B	8
A	2

A	2
B	8

8	A
B	2

(a)   (b)   (c)   (d)

Answers: 1. (c); **2.** (a); **3.** (d); **4.** (d); **5.** (a); **6.** (d); **7.** (b); **8.** (a); **9.** (b); **10.** (a); **11.** (b); **12.** (b); **13.** (a); **14.** (b); **15.** (b); **16.** (b); **17.** (c); **18.** (a); **19.** (a); **20.** (b); **21.** (d); **22.** (b); **23.** (a); **24.** (d); **25.** (a); **26.** (b); **27.** (c); **28.** (a); **29.** (b); **30.** (a).

Strategic Thinking Test

In each of the following strategic thinking questions you need to select your objective, and then decide which of the suggested possible courses of action best helps you to meet your objective. Circle your chosen answer. The 'correct' answers follow the test, but remember that in real life, how you go about answering questions like these may be as important as the answer you finally choose. You may be given the chance to expand upon your thinking process after the test, and so often no single correct answer exists.

An alternative way for you to attempt these tests is to place the various options you've been given in preferred order of priority. Try answering questions in both ways. Clarity of thinking and structured decision making is more important in this test than simply choosing the correct answer.

This test has no time limit, but you should complete all five sections within an hour at the most.

1. The Production Line

You are a production manager for a large manufacturing company. You arrive at work early on a Monday morning and see that the production line has stopped. Your shift

manager tells you that an electrical fault on a packaging machine at the end of the line caused a fire that the Fire Service crews, who are still on site, put out. Production has stopped until the maintenance crew can repair the damage.

Raw materials are still being delivered by your suppliers, who face a large fine from you if they are late with deliveries. Packaging materials are also still being delivered to the machine that had the fire.

You have a large delivery to make later that morning to one of your biggest customers. You can't possibly make it. The day shift has arrived and are milling around the plant with nothing to do. Officers from the Health and Safety Executive (HSE) have just arrived and want to begin an investigation immediately.

(i) What is your objective?

(a) Ensure that customers are notified of the delay.

(b) Ensure the safety of the workers on site.

(c) Get production going as quickly as possible.

(ii) What is your preferred course of action?

(a) Ask the workers to leave the plant.

(b) Ask the fire crews to confirm that the fire is out.

(c) Tell the repair crew to start work immediately.

(d) Take the HSE staff to the site of the fire.

(e) Call your suppliers to tell them to stop deliveries.

(f) Check the fire is out yourself.

(g) Move the packaging materials from the site of the fire.

2. The Flooded Village

Recent heavy rains have left a village cut off from the outside world. You are in charge of the emergency effort. A call from one of the people in the village indicates that there have been a few casualties, although none of them are serious at the moment. Food supplies are running low, and the village runs out of fresh water in 12 hours. Several elderly people are trapped alone in their houses, as are a number of families with young children.

The flood water should subside within 24 hours.

You have three off-road vehicles, a fleet of small boats, and a transport helicopter at your disposal.

(i) What is your objective?

(a) Rescue the elderly people and young children.

(b) Get fresh water into the village.

(c) Get food and medical supplies into the village.

(ii) What is your preferred course of action?

(a) Use the boats to rescue the elderly people and young children immediately.

(b) Try to use the off-road vehicles to get through the flood water with food and medical supplies.

(c) Wait for the flood water to subside, and then launch a full-scale relief effort.

(d) Use the helicopter to fly fresh water into the village.

(e) Use the helicopter to rescue the trapped people from their houses.

(f) Use the boats to rescue the casualties.

(g) Use the helicopter to fly medical personnel into the village.

3. The Defectors

You are a senior manager within your company. You arrive at work one morning to find a letter addressed to you from your managing director (MD) announcing that he has gone to work for your largest competitor. His contract states that he must give three months' notice. He hasn't done this. You know he has confidential knowledge relating to your customers, and has known many of them personally for years.

An hour later, his personal assistant calls in to say she is also resigning to go with her old boss to his new employer. She tells you that she thinks the marketing director has also defected to your competitor.

With key members of the senior management team gone, you need to act quickly.

(i) What is your objective?

(a) Prevent your managing director from using any confidential customer information to your disadvantage.

(b) Protect your customer base.

(c) Appoint replacements for the missing senior personnel.

(ii) What is your preferred course of action?

(a) Try to locate the marketing director.

(b) Write to your customers telling them what has happened, and that they are contractually obliged to still use your company as a supplier.

(c) Write to your customers telling them what has happened, thank them for their business thus far, and restate your commitment to good customer service.

(d) Write to your customers telling them what has happened, and that you will shortly be cutting costs to remain their preferred supplier.

(e) Threaten your MD with legal action for not honoring his contract.

(f) Call the MD and try to persuade him to come back.

(g) Call your biggest customers, thank them for their business thus far, and restate your commitment to good customer service.

4. The Building Site

You are building a home for your family that is almost completed. You arrive at the building site one morning for a routine visit to find no work being carried out. One of the builders tells you that your project manager, whose job is to manage and pay all the workers, has been called away on urgent family business and has left no instructions for the workers on site.

The house is without power and water supplies. Workers from the electricity and water supply companies are on site waiting to connect the house to water and electricity supplies. They tell you that if they can't start work within the next couple of hours they have to leave for their next job, and they aren't sure when they'll be able to call again.

The electrician tells you that his work is almost complete, but he refuses to do any further work because he hasn't been paid by the project manager for the work done so far. The plumber is also waiting for materials, which your project manager was supposed to have arranged for delivery to the site today, but so far nothing has arrived. You also notice that none of the doors and windows has had locks fitted.

As you are wondering what to do, the Local Authority Building Standards and Regulations Officer arrives to carry out a routine inspection.

You have sold your current home, and you and your family have to vacate it within the week.

(i) What is your objective?

(a) Make sure that the house is secure.

(b) Make sure that the house is safe.

(c) Make sure that the water and electricity supplies are finally connected.

(ii) What is your preferred course of action?

(a) Book a hotel for you and your family to stay in.

(b) Order what the plumber needs yourself, and tell the plumber and electrician to complete their work and you'll bear any costs directly.

(c) Ask the Building Standards and Regulations Officer to come back the next day.

(d) Tell the Building Standards and Regulations Officer to begin his inspection.

(e) Start to fit window and door locks yourself.

(f) Call the project manager to find out what's going on.

(g) Order the plumbing supplies by phone, and ask the supplier to invoice the project manager.

5. The In Tray

This question is slightly different. Instead of choosing from a set of objectives and preferred actions, you need to specify your objective yourself, and prioritise a list of potential actions.

You work for a firm of engineering consultants. When you arrive at work this morning, you are faced with the following:

(a) The post is waiting to be opened.

(b) You need to check your e-mail.

(c) A document from the marketing director, marked 'urgent', is waiting to be faxed to a customer.

(d) The fax machine has no paper.

(e) Your assistant has called in sick. She left a message saying that there are some invoices on her desk, which need to be checked and posted today.

(f) Someone is in reception. He says he has an appointment with a member of your staff.

(g) There is no coffee, but the canteen is downstairs.

(h) Your answer phone contains a message from the managing director. He says his car has broken down and he's going to be late for a 10.00 a.m. meeting with a client. He wants you to call and let the client know.

(i) What is your objective?

_____

(ii) In what order would you tackle the above tasks? Write a few words about why you have chosen to prioritise the tasks the way you have.

_____

_____

_____

_____

_____

_____

Answers: Remember that no 'correct' answers actually exist in these types of test, and that your preferred courses of action change with the initial objective you choose. So, here I tell you what I would do in these scenarios, along with a few words about why I chose these options.

1. The Production Line

Safety seems to me to be the over-riding issue here, so I choose (b) as my objective. Because the fire crews are on site, and probably in control of the situation, I choose (b) as my preferred action, because I can get going with the rest of the tasks when I know the fire is out and the site is safe. I don't allow anyone near the site of the fire until the professionals say that doing so is safe. I just have to accept that production must stop when factories have incidents like this.

2. The Flooded Village

My first objective here is to ensure the safety of people, so I choose objective (a). I think everything else can safely wait for a while until the water subsides. As the helicopter takes too long, and the vehicles have no guarantee of getting through, I choose (a) as my preferred course of action.

3. The Defectors

Here, I choose (b) as my objective. Protecting my customer base is a positive rather than a negative action, and focuses on the lifeblood of any business – its customers. Rather than making threats, and not wanting to appear panicky by cutting prices, I choose (g) as my course of action. I also think that calling is more personal than sending a letter.

4. The Building Site

We need somewhere to live! So I choose (b) as my objective. I can live somewhere without water or electricity, but not if the roof is in danger of collapsing! Consequently, I choose (d) as my course of action. However, I almost chose objective (c) and (b) or (c) as my course of action.

5. The In Tray

I decide that customer service is my objective, so I choose my priorities on that basis and deal with the most urgent customer issues first. Then I deal with what is left in order of the next most important thing – cash flow. Here is my order of priorities:

> 1. (h) and (f), in case the person in reception is a customer;
>
> 2. (d), because filling the machine with paper only takes a minute and means I can do (c) next;
>
> 3. (c) and (g), so that I can give my reception guest, who may be a customer, a cup of coffee;
>
> 4. (a), in case the post contains any cheques!;
>
> 5. (e), so that we can get paid;
>
> 6. (b), because the information I have to hand suggests that this action has the least immediate impact on my objectives.

Chapter 13

Technical Ability Sample Tests

● ●

In This Chapter

▶ Measuring your mechanical ability

▶ Checking out your spatial ability

▶ Assessing your accuracy

▶ Finding the answers

● ●

*T*his chapter gets you into technical ability tests. You can just dip in and have a quick look or try the complete tests using the time limits shown in Table 13–1.

Table 13–1   Technical Ability Sample Test Time Limits

Type of Test	Time Limit
Mechanical Ability Test	**20 minutes**
Spatial Ability Speed Test	**20 minutes**
Spatial Ability Power Tests	
Rotating Three-Dimensional Objects	25 minutes
Constructing Three-Dimensional Objects	30 minutes
Detail and Accuracy Speed Tests	
Test 1	5 minutes
Test 2	10 minutes
Detail and Accuracy Power Test	**15 minutes**

You can find the correct answers at the end of each test.

Mechanical Ability Test

Read each of the mechanical ability questions that follow. Circle what you consider to be the correct answers.

1. Each vessel contains 1 litre of water. Which drains the quickest?

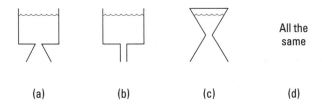

(a)   (b)   (c)   (d)

2. Each object is 1 metre tall. Which has the largest surface area?

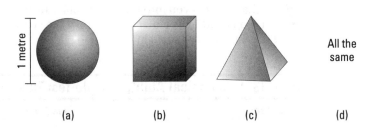

(a)   (b)   (c)   (d)

3. Which set of bulbs produces the most light?

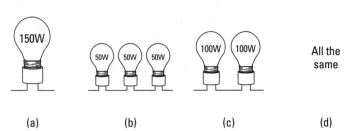

(a)   (b)   (c)   (d)

4. Three cannons fire three identical cannonballs. Each travels at the same velocity. Which hits the ground first?

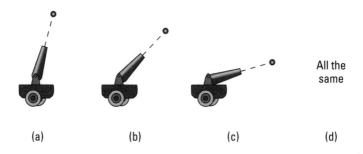

<table>
<tr><td>(a)</td><td>(b)</td><td>(c)</td><td>All the
same
(d)</td></tr>
</table>

5. Which train has the least load per wheel?

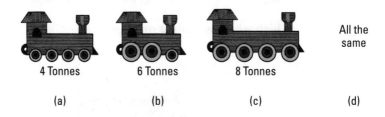

4 Tonnes	6 Tonnes	8 Tonnes	All the same
(a)	(b)	(c)	(d)

6. You are standing somewhere in the northern hemisphere looking south. At noon the sun is always directly south.

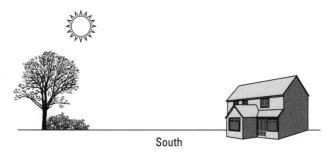

South

Is it now (a) morning or (b) afternoon?

7. Which planet is moving fastest?

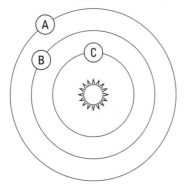

(a) Planet A   (b) Planet B

(c) Planet C   (d) All moving at the same speed

8. Which wheel is turning quickest?

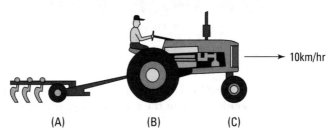

10km/hr

(A)   (B)   (C)

(a) Wheel A   (b) Wheel B

(c) Wheel C   (d) All moving at the same speed

9. Heat is applied to a metal bar as shown. Which shape does the bar initially take?

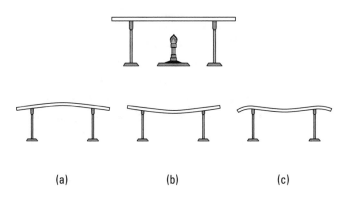

(a)   (b)   (c)

10. Opening which window causes this greenhouse to cool the quickest?

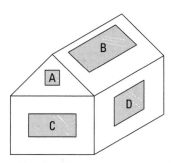

(a) Window A   (b) Window B
(c) Window C   (d) Window D

11. Where does box Z end up?

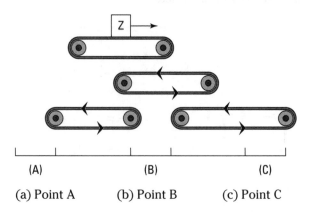

(a) Point A   (b) Point B   (c) Point C

12. Which loudspeaker produces the deepest sound?

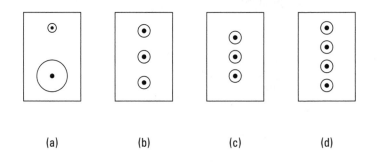

(a)   (b)   (c)   (d)

13. Which hammer is most likely to break the rock?

(a) Hammer A   (b) Hammer B
(c) Hammer C   (d) All the same

14. A train joins a one-way track at point P. Which junction must fit at point Y to allow the train to travel the whole track before leaving at point S?

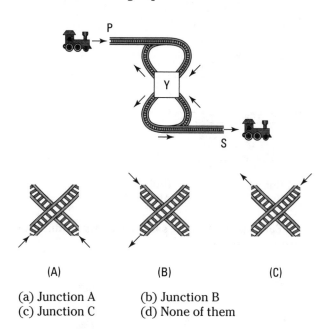

(A)   (B)   (C)

(a) Junction A   (b) Junction B
(c) Junction C   (d) None of them

15. Each vessel of water can fill exactly six glasses. Which has the largest volume?

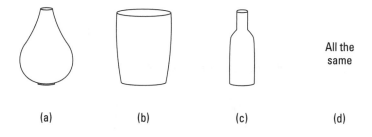

All the
same

(a)   (b)   (c)   (d)

16. Which bulb glows the brightest?

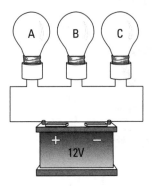

(a) Bulb A   (b) Bulb B
(c) Bulb C   (d) All the same

17. Each spring has the same breaking strain. Which stretches the most?

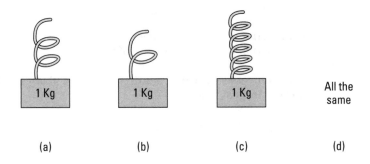

(a)   (b)   (c)   (d)

18. Which star is the largest?

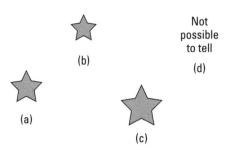

19. Which boat displaces the most water?

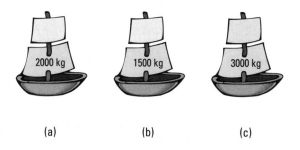

(a) (b) (c)

20. A record is playing at 33 rpm. Which point on the record is moving the fastest?

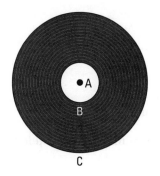

(a) Point A (b) Point B
(c) Point C (d) All the same

21. Wheels P, Q, and R are identical. For one revolution of P, Q, and R, which wheel from A, B, or C turns the most?

(a) Wheel A (b) Wheel B
(c) Wheel C (d) All the same

22. Which container holds the densest fluid?

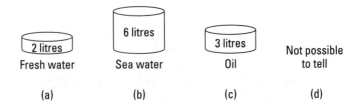

2 litres	6 litres	3 litres	Not possible
Fresh water	Sea water	Oil	to tell
(a)	(b)	(c)	(d)

23. If the spouts A, B, and C were opened at the same time, from which would water flow the quickest?

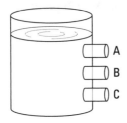

(a) Spout A   (b) Spout B
(c) Spout C   (d) All the same

24. At which point is the pendulum moving quickest?

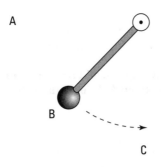

(a) Point A   (b) Point B
(c) Point C   (d) All the same

25. Which bag is heaviest?

(a) Bag X   (b) Bag Y
(c) Both the same   (d) Can't tell

26. Which direction does wheel Y turn?

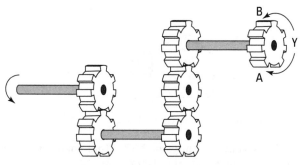

(a) Direction A   (b) Direction B

27. Which bicycle is easiest to pedal uphill?

(A)   (B)

(a) Bicycle A   (b) Bicycle B   (c) Both the same

28. Which pair of magnets attract each other?

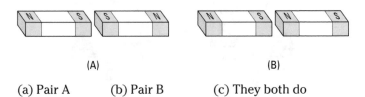

(A)   (B)

(a) Pair A   (b) Pair B   (c) They both do

29. As the sun rises, the shadow cast by the house. . .

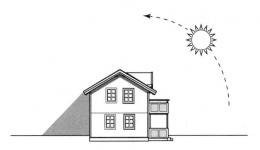

(a) Gets longer   (b) Gets shorter   (c) Stays the same

30. Two runners approach the final corner of a racetrack at the same speed, which finishes first?

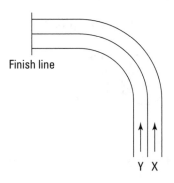

Finish line

Y X

(a) Runner X   (b) Runner Y   (c) Both finish at the same time

Answers: 1. (d); **2.** (b); **3.** (c); **4.** (c); **5.** (a); **6.** (a); **7.** (c); **8.** (a); **9.** (b); **10.** (b); **11.** (a); **12.** (a); **13.** (c); **14.** (c); **15.** (d); **16.** (d); **17.** (c); **18.** (d); **19.** (c); **20.** (c); **21.** (b); **22.** (c); **23.** (c); **24.** (c); **25.** (d); **26.** (a); **27.** (a); **28.** (b); **29.** (b); **30.** (b).

Spatial Ability Speed Test

This spatial ability speed test asks you to look at the rotation of two-dimensional objects. You need to look at the first object, and then choose from those that follow which one you think is the same. Circle what you consider to be the correct answer.

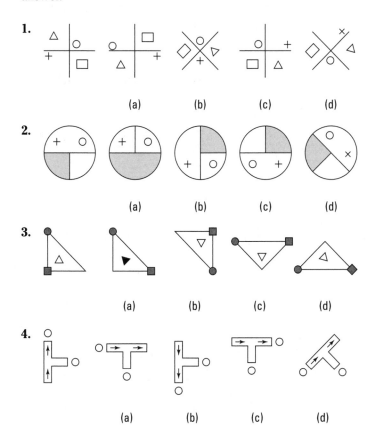

1.

        (a)   (b)   (c)   (d)

2.

        (a)   (b)   (c)   (d)

3.

        (a)   (b)   (c)   (d)

4.

        (a)   (b)   (c)   (d)

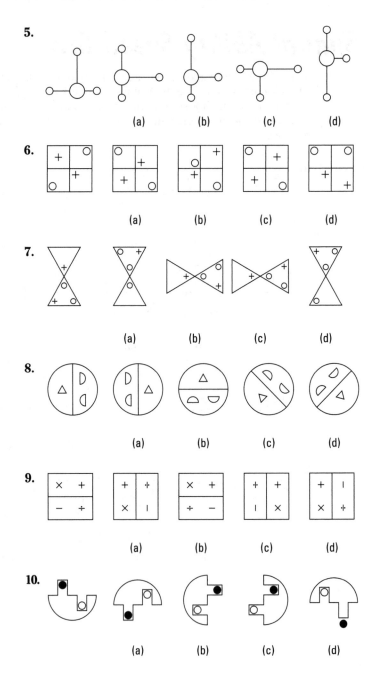

5.

    (a)   (b)   (c)   (d)

6.

    (a)   (b)   (c)   (d)

7.

    (a)   (b)   (c)   (d)

8.

    (a)   (b)   (c)   (d)

9.

    (a)   (b)   (c)   (d)

10.

    (a)   (b)   (c)   (d)

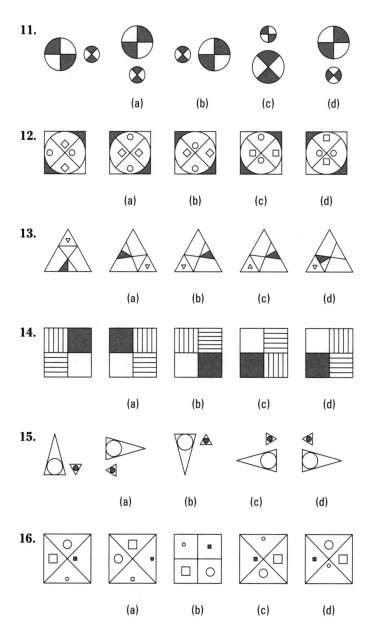

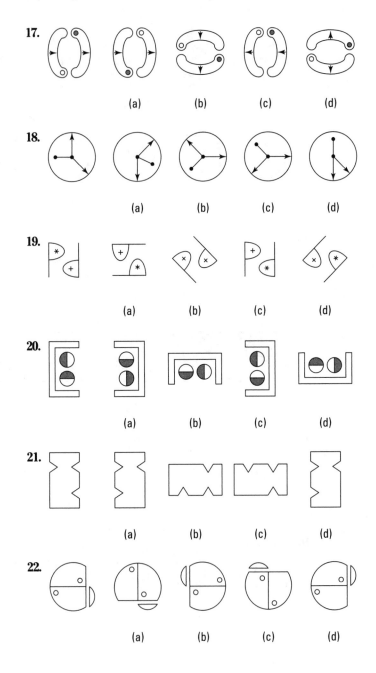

17.

(a)　　　(b)　　　(c)　　　(d)

18.

(a)　　　(b)　　　(c)　　　(d)

19.

(a)　　　(b)　　　(c)　　　(d)

20.

(a)　　　(b)　　　(c)　　　(d)

21.

(a)　　　(b)　　　(c)　　　(d)

22.

(a)　　　(b)　　　(c)　　　(d)

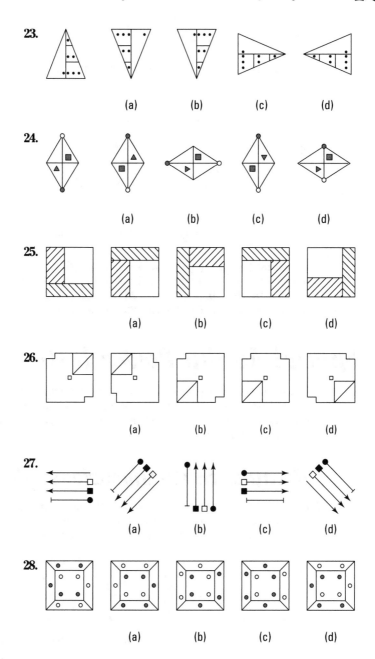

29.

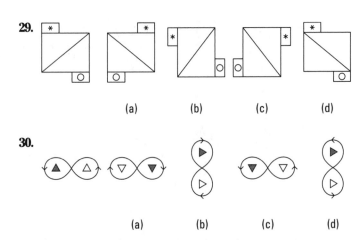

        (a)   (b)   (c)   (d)

30.

        (a)   (b)   (c)   (d)

Answers: 1. (d); **2.** (c); **3.** (b); **4.** (c); **5.** (a); **6.** (a); **7.** (b); **8.** (c); **9.** (a); **10.** (b); **11.** (d); **12.** (b); **13.** (b); **14.** (c); **15.** (a); **16.** (c); **17.** (b); **18.** (b); **19.** (c); **20.** (a); **21.** (b); **22.** (b); **23.** (c); **24.** (c); **25.** (c); **26.** (b); **27.** (d); **28.** (a); **29.** (c); **30.** (d).

Spatial Ability Power Tests

These spatial ability power tests are more complex than the speed tests, mainly because you need to consider three dimensions when visualising the object. You may find they take more effort to complete.

Rotating three-dimensional objects

In this rotation test you must look at the first object, and then choose from those that follow which one you think is the same. Circle what you consider to be the correct answer.

1.

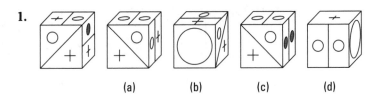

        (a)   (b)   (c)   (d)

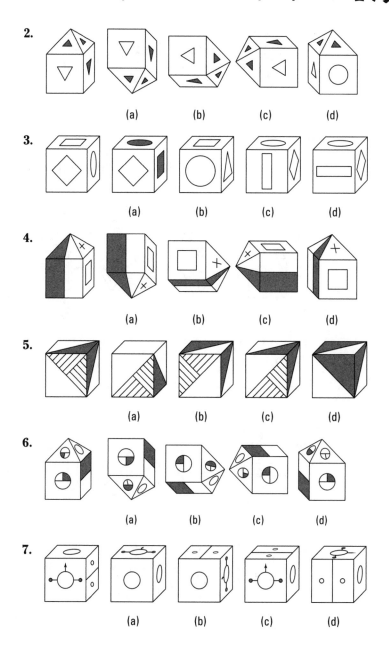

2.

    (a)   (b)   (c)   (d)

3.

    (a)   (b)   (c)   (d)

4.

    (a)   (b)   (c)   (d)

5.

    (a)   (b)   (c)   (d)

6.

    (a)   (b)   (c)   (d)

7.

    (a)   (b)   (c)   (d)

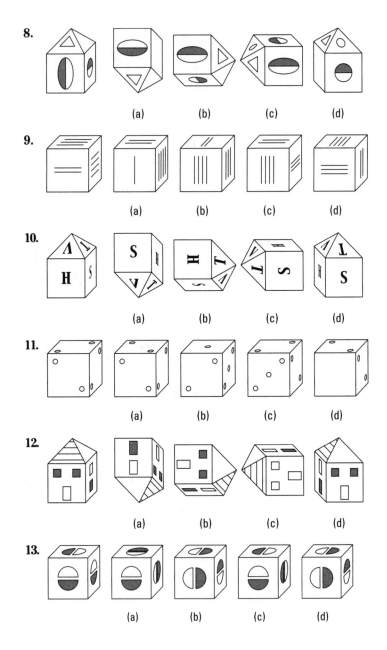

8.

    (a)   (b)   (c)   (d)

9.

    (a)   (b)   (c)   (d)

10.

    (a)   (b)   (c)   (d)

11.

    (a)   (b)   (c)   (d)

12.

    (a)   (b)   (c)   (d)

13.

    (a)   (b)   (c)   (d)

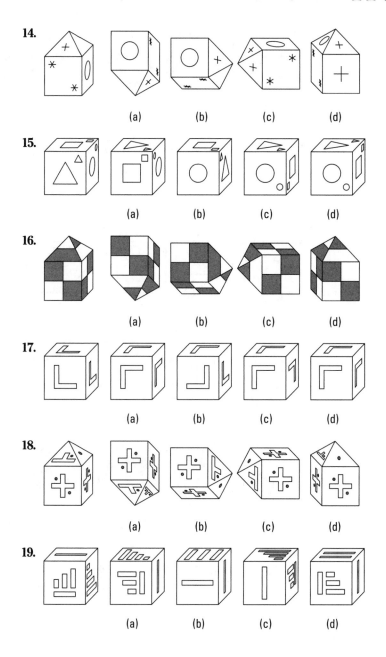

14.

(a)   (b)   (c)   (d)

15.

(a)   (b)   (c)   (d)

16.

(a)   (b)   (c)   (d)

17.

(a)   (b)   (c)   (d)

18.

(a)   (b)   (c)   (d)

19.

(a)   (b)   (c)   (d)

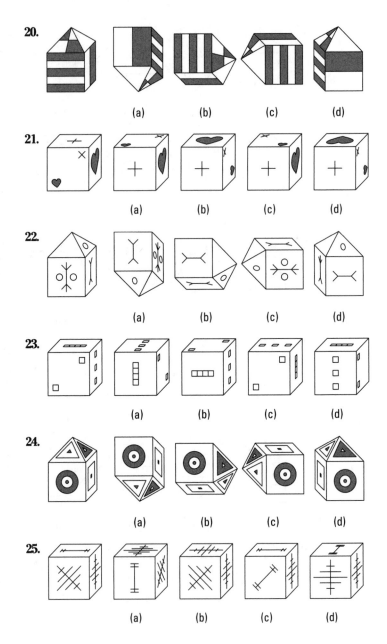

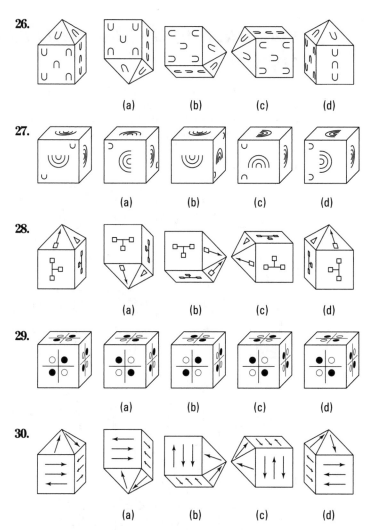

Answers: 1. (b); **2.** (b); **3.** (c); **4.** (c); **5.** (a); **6.** (c); **7.** (d); **8.** (b); **9.** (a); **10.** (d); **11.** (d); **12.** (a); **13.** (a); **14.** (a); **15.** (c); **16.** (b); **17.** (c); **18.** (b); **19.** (c); **20.** (b); **21.** (d); **22.** (a); **23.** (a); **24.** (c); **25.** (a); **26.** (b); **27.** (d); **28.** (c); **29.** (c); **30.** (a).

Constructing three-dimensional objects

In this construction test you need to look at the unfolded shape, and then choose which of the objects that follow would best represent the first object if it were folded. Circle what you consider to be the correct answer.

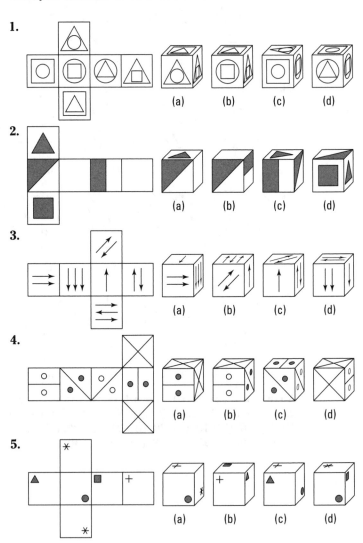

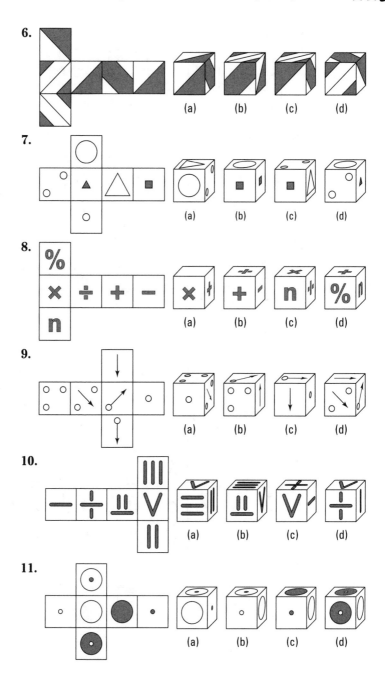

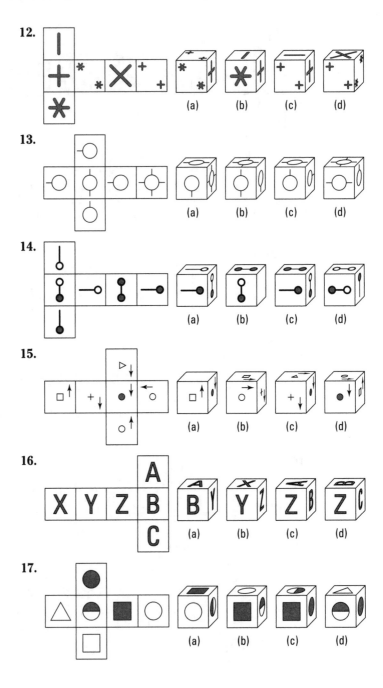

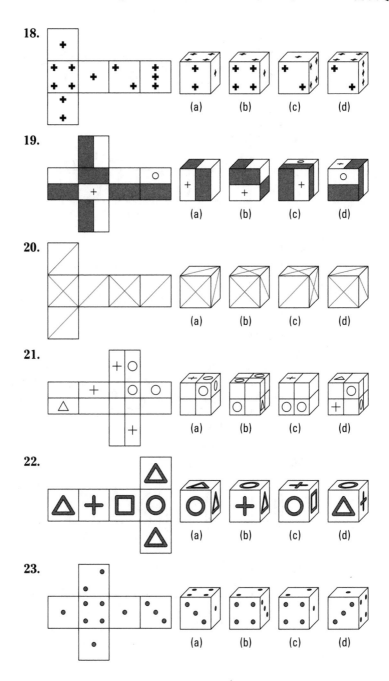

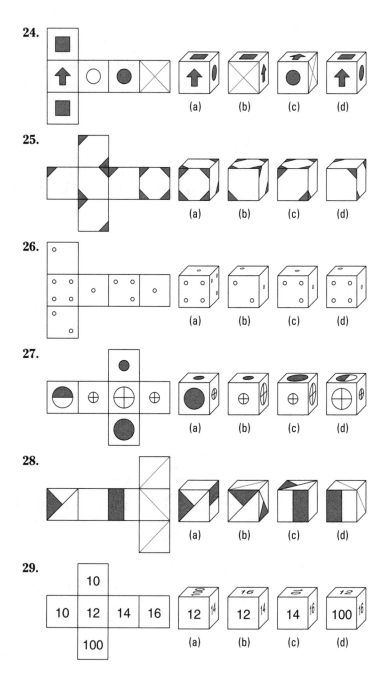

30.

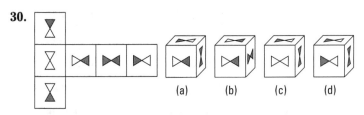

(a)   (b)   (c)   (d)

Answers: 1. (c); **2.** (a); **3.** (c); **4.** (b); **5.** (d); **6.** (a); **7.** (d); **8.** (c); **9.** (d); **10.** (b); **11.** (b); **12.** (c); **13.** (c); **14.** (a); **15.** (c); **16.** (c); **17.** (c); **18.** (a); **19.** (b); **20.** (a); **21.** (a); **22.** (a); **23.** (c); **24.** (b); **25.** (b); **26.** (d); **27.** (b); **28.** (d); **29.** (c); **30.** (b).

Detail and Accuracy Speed Tests

Detail and accuracy speed tests are some of the most challenging psychometric tests you can come across. They require prolonged concentration because you have to take in a lot of information very quickly, and work at a fine level of detail.

Test 1

Your task here is to compare the information in the first and second columns. Draw a line under the information in the second column if you find any differences between them.

1.	6jls8sqqvl	6jlss8qqvl
2.	44487555yn	44485755yn
3.	rndd955ijr	rnddd55ijr
4.	sireeem1rt	sireeem1rt
5.	dddotplba5	ddpotplba5
6.	333orhh86n	333orhh86h
7.	eeeon5ithh	eeeon5ithh
8.	sott09qrqr	sott09trqr
9.	aaaot75yhh	Aaa5t7yyhh
10.	0077nurmkk	0077nurmkk
11.	ssp660256f	ssp660256f

12.	bbbjriyyp2	bbbjriyyp2
13.	aasirt336s	aasrit336s
14.	nnvutommvn	nnvutomvmn
15.	dddhvxxsww	dddhxvxsww
16.	njvvmornq2	njvvmorn92
17.	dddi44kgnt	dddi44kqnt
18.	plwwbqaa99	plwwbqaa99
19.	cccntlllin	cccntlllin
20.	fiiitnooyi	fiittnooyi
21.	qhu48gst32	qhu48gst32
22.	hjhi7pply7	hjhi7pply7
23.	ssso993fqq	ssxo993fqq
24.	cbjqplmaez	cbjqplmeaz
25.	006nisnnww	006ninsnww
26.	aaffeerasa	aaffeerasa
27.	pqrqpqpqqr	ppqrqppqqr
28.	p660bdpq56	p660bdpq56
29.	cclorbitty	cclorbitty
30.	msnsvyyebs	msnsvyvebs
31.	11it1it1it	11it1itiit
32.	d6d66qqn69	d66ddqqn69
33.	bpqbbpq96p	bpqbbpq96q
34.	zxzyeeo257	zyzyeeo257
35.	2zz22t7t27	2zz22l7t27
36.	opqqqdop06	opqqqdop06
37.	io844ghhwf	io84g4hhwf
38.	fftfty7fql	fftftf7fql

39.	cocq49cb11	copq49cb11
40.	uui8776rer	uui8776rer

Answers: Differences are present in items **1**; **2**; **3**; **5**; **6**; **8**; **9**; **13**; **14**; **15**; **16**; **17**; **20**; **23**; **24**; **25**; **27**; **30**; **31**; **32**; **33**; **34**; **35**; **37**; **38**; **39**.

Test 2

In this second detail and accuracy speed test you need to read the first data set and identify the correct copy from the answer options that follow. Circle your chosen answer. If you think none of the options are correct, choose answer option (d)('none of them').

1. 7388457544

(a) 7384575547   (b) 7388477547
(c) 738447547   (d) None of them

2. 456E7ff45g

(a) 456E7ffe5g   (b) 456E7ef45g
(c) 454E7ff45g   (d) None of them

3. FfF445sd55

(a) FFf445sd55   (b) fFF445sd55
(c) FFF445sd55   (d) None of them

4. Nkdd45622w

(a) Nkd45622v   (b) Nkdd4562w
(c) Nkd45622w   (d) None of them

5. Hqilebbsha

(a) Hqilebbsha   (b) Hqilebsha
(c) Hqiebbsha   (d) None of them

6. Vnvmmwbbbs

(a) Vnvmwbsbs   (b) Vnvmmwbis
(c) Vnvimwbbs   (d) None of them

7. Sst6555sts

(a) Sst655Ssts   (b) Sst6S55sts
(c) Sst6555sts   (d) None of them

8. Bbburu9bcb

(a) BburB9bcb   (b) Bbburu9bcb
(c) BbburB9cb   (d) None of them

9. 11hii1t6ty1

(a) 11hii1t6ty1   (b) 1lhii1t6ty1
(c) 11hiilt6ty1   (d) None of them

10. xhXxvhvh

(a) xhXHxvhvh   (b) xhXVxvhvh
(c) xhXHvhvh   (d) None of them

11. nnvnnvvnmn

(a) nnvnnvvnmn   (b) nnvnnvvnn
(c) nnnnvvnmn   (d) None of them

12. huytyYvtyu

(a) huytyYvtvu   (b) huvtyYvtyu
(c) huytyYvtyu   (d) None of them

13. wvvnvVvw7w

(a) wvvVvv7w   (b) vvvnvVvw7w
(c) vvnvVv7w   (d) None of them

14. nnvwyWgg39

(a) nvwyWgg39   (b) nvwyWg39
(c) nnvyWgg39   (d) None of them

15. 8226777tf7

(a) 8226777tf7   (b) 8226677tf7
(c) 8266777tf7   (d) None of them

16. 1887856568

(a) 188786568   (b) 1887856568
(c) 188756568   (d) None of them

17. ageTTeftef

(a) ageTTetfef   (b) ageTTefetf
(c) ageTTeftef   (d) None of them

18. vbsUhwokok

(a) vbsUhwkok   (b) vbsUhwook
(c) vbsUhwokok   (d) None of them

19. lllttti77i

(a) lllttti7i7i   (b) llltiti77i
(c) lllttti77i   (d) None of them

20. asarrqeaar

(a) asarqreaar   (b) asarrqeaar
(c) assrrqeaar   (d) None of them

21. tlTa7t7aly

(a) tlTa7l7aly   (b) tlTa7t7aly
(c) tlTL7t7aly   (d) None of them

22. cCvyYywgtt

(a) cCvyYyygtt   (b) ctvytywgtt
(c) cCvYywgtt   (d) None of them

23. 4467te66t5

(a) 4467te66t5   (b) 4467t6e6t5
(c) 44e67te66t5   (d) None of them

24. nh111771tt

(a) nh117171tt   (b) nh171771tt
(c) nh111771tt   (d) None of them

25. uiouuiounu

(a) uiouuioinu   (b) uiouuiounu
(c) uiouoiounu   (d) None of them

26. vgd53udv35

(a) vgd53dv35   (b) vgd35udv35
(c) vg53dudv35   (d) None of them

27. nwt5888715

(a) nwt588715   (b) nwt5888175
(c) nw5888715   (d) None of them

28. bnhbhbhnhb

(a) bnhbhbhnhb   (b) bnhbhhnhb
(c) bnbhbhnhb   (d) None of them

29. tywttwtyty

(a) tywtwttyty   (b) tywttwtyty
(c) tywytwtyty   (d) None of them

30. 8847487775

(a) 8847478775   (b) 884787775
(c) 8847487775   (d) None of them

31. njsSyjyjTy

(a) njsSyjjyTy   (b) njsSyijyTy
(c) njsySjyjTy   (d) None of them

32. klttkLKtkt

(a) klttkLKtkt   (b) kltktLKtkt
(c) klttkLKktt   (d) None of them

33. aaNn5a552a

(a) aaNn5a252a   (b) aanN5a552a
(c) anN5a552a   (d) None of them

34. njjjnjnjnn

(a) njjjnjnjnj
(c) njnjnjnjnn

(b) njjjnnjjnn
(d) None of them

35. qpqppqppqq

(a) qpqpqppqq
(c) qpqpaqppqq

(b) qpqpPqppqq
(d) None of them

36. 1117771551

(a) 111771551
(c) 111775551

(b) 1117171551
(d) None of them

37. nnwnwnmmnn

(a) nnwnvnmnn
(c) nnwnnmvnn

(b) nnnvwnmnn
(d) None of them

38. 0910996696

(a) 091096696
(c) 0910996696

(b) 0910696696
(d) None of them

39. huvhhvuhuh

(a) huvhvvuhuh
(c) huvhhvuhuh

(b) huvhvuhuh
(d) None of them

40. xxvzzvzvzv

(a) xxvzzvzvzv
(c) xxvzxvzvzv

(b) xxvzvvzvzv
(d) None of them

Answers: 1. (d); **2.** (d); **3.** (d); **4.** (d); **5.** (a); **6.** (d); **7.** (c); **8.** (b);
9. (a); **10.** (d); **11.** (a); **12.** (c); **13.** (d); **14.** (d); **15.** (a); **16.** (b);
17. (c); **18.** (c); **19.** (c); **20.** (b); **21.** (b); **22.** (d); **23.** (a); **24.** (c);
25. (b); **26.** (d); **27.** (d); **28.** (a); **29.** (b); **30.** (c); **31.** (d); **32.** (a);
33. (d); **34.** (d); **35.** (d); **36.** (d); **37.** (d); **38.** (c); **39.** (c); **40.** (a).

Detail and Accuracy Power Test

Your task in this detail and accuracy power test is to compare the information in the first and second columns. Circle any differences you find between them in the second column.

---

1. E.M Watham
   56 Cherry Ave.
   Godalming, Surrey
   T/F - 7777867
   CRef WAS444653
   PdOrd :HS1-331
   PO:Name as Ref.
   RP : Y

   E.M Watham
   56 Cherry Ave.
   Godalming, Surrey
   T/F - 7777867
   CRef WAS444653
   PdOrd :HS1331
   PO:Name as Ref.
   RP : Y

---

2. Mr S. Roedean
   Box 9001
   Sunderland
   Tyne and Wear
   T/F - n/a
   Customer Ref - SUN243477/C
   Pd Ord :n/a
   PO No: n/a
   RP : N

   Mr S. Roedean
   Box 9001
   Sunderland
   Tyne and Wear
   T/F - n/a
   Customer Ref - SUN243477/C
   Pd Ord :n/a
   PO No: n/a
   RP : N

---

3. Emily Banard
   Flat B, Harton Moore Lane.
   Leicester
   PostCode Needed
   T/F - not given
   Customer Ref - LES43366[New]
   Pd Ord :SW9 2497 x 21
   PO No: Name as Ref.
   RP : N

   Emily Banard
   Flat B, Harton More Lane.
   Leicester
   PostCode Needed
   T/F - not given
   Customer Ref - LES43366(New)
   Pd Ord :SW9 2497 x 21
   PO No: Name as Ref.
   RP : N

---

4. Mr J Burke
   119 New York Ave.
   Bristol
   T/F - 5598565
   Customer Ref - TBS12153
   Pd Ord WY113
   PO No: Bu001
   RP : Y

   Mr J Burke
   19 New York Ave.
   Bristol
   T/F - 5598565
   Customer Ref - TBS12153
   Pd Ord WY113
   PO No: Bu001
   RP : N

---

5. Mrs W. McInery
5 Hope Street.
Berwick -upon Tweed,
Berwickhire
T/F - 1753339 (mob)
Customer Ref - BTS35977
Pd Ord :- GH17879
[Check this please?]
PO No: Cust Name.
RP : N

Mrs W. McInery
5 Hope Street.
Berwick -upon Tweed,
Berwickhire
T/F - 1753339 (mb
Customer Ref - BTS35977
Pd Ord :- GH17879
[Check this please]
PO No: Cust Name.
RP : N

6. Mrs Y Gainford Hensfield Rd
West Yorks
T/F - 783644
Customer Ref - WYS11443
Pd Ord :- DR16 125
PO No: TG22
RP : Y

Mrs Y Gainsford Hensfield Rd
West Yorks
T/F - 783644
Customer Ref - WYS11443
Pd Ord :- DR16 125
PO No: TG22
RP : Y

7. H. Garth
12 (?) Eden Cres.
Hurworth.
Southampton
T/F - n/a try email
Customer Ref - non-allocated
Pd Ord :- CW5-2261
PO No: HGX
RP : N

H. Garth
12 (?) Eden Cres.
Hurworth.
Southampton
T/F - n/a email
Customer Ref - non-allocted
Pd Ord :- CW5-2261
PO No: HGX
RP : N

8. Miss OH George
86 Deneside Road.
Snotterton, Worcs
T/F - none
Customer Ref - EGY2765 .
Pd Ord :- JKP1-23
PO No: OHG ?
RP : N

Miss OH George
86 Deneside Road.
Snotterton, Worcs
T/F - none
Customer Ref - EGY2765
Pd Ord :- JKP1-23
PO No: OHG ?
RP : N

9. Mr GG Hargreave
Four Ends House
Rowanburn, Merseyside
T/F - 235568 (mb)
Customer Ref - RB23421PC
Pd Ord :- AZ1 -2477
PO No: Cust Name
RP : Yes

Mr GG Hargreave
Four Ends House
Rowanburn, Merseyside
T/F - 235568 (mob)
Customer Ref - RB23421PC
Pd Ord :- A21 -2477
PO No: Cust Name
RP : Yes

10.	Mr B Allen	Mr B Allen
	29 Hemmel House Rd	29 Hemmel House Rd
	Lyndale, Bucks	Lyndale, Bucks
	T/F - n/a use email	TF - n/a use email
	Customer Ref - QAK23876	Customer Ref - QAK23876
	Prd Ord : GHY5 x 3	Prd Ord : GHY5 - 3
	PO No: BAL	Po No: BAL
	RP : Y	RP : Y
11.	S M Riding	S M Riding
	12b Hollycroft House.	12b Hollycroft House.
	Ashmount, Herts	Ashmount, Herts
	T/F - 4998578	T/F - 4998578
	Customer Ref - SRI2311	Customer Ref - SRI2311
	Pd Od : JR316 (none)	Pd Od : JR316 (one)
	[Not in stock, please call]	[Not in stock, please call]
	PO No: Name as Ref.	PO No: Name as Ref.
	RP : N	RP : N
12.	Mr (N?) Cowals	Mr (N?) Cowals
	63 Kings Head Road.	63 Kings Head Road.
	Brompton, Exeter	Brompton, Exeter
	T/F - 5488795	T/F - 5488795
	[Wrong phone no.]	[Wrong phone no.]
	Cust Ref - BNB453	Cust Ref - BNB453
	Pd Ord :- TYR598	Pd Ord :- TYR598
	PO No: NCO. ??	PO No: NCO.
	RP : N	RP : N
13.	Mrs E. Tenby	Mrs E. Tenby
	Glenmount	Glenmount
	Fendene, Clara Vale	Feldene, Clara Vale
	T/F - 15777984 (mob)	T/F - 15777984 (mob)
	Customer Ref - ETE4776	Customer Ref - ET4776
	Prod :- HJS2311	Prod :- HJS2311
	PO No: ETE.	PO No: ETE.
	RP : N	RP : Y
14.	Miss W. Marlbry	Miss W. Marlbry
	22 Reasby Hall Rd.	22 Reasby Hall Rd.
	Hillcrest, London S12	Hillcrest, London S2
	T/F - 2358794	T/F - 2358794
	Customer Ref - MAR1	Customer Ref - MAR
	Pd Ord :- No Order	Pd Ord :- No Order
	PO No: Cust name	PO No: Cust name
	RP : Y	RP : Y

15. Mrs TY Langcliffe 17a Pinecroft (Ave?). Galadale, Ayrshire T/F - 5487542 Customer Ref - GAL457 Pd Ord :- HT11234 PO No: TYL. RP : N	Mrs TY Langcliffe 17 Pincroft (Ave?). Galadale, Ayrshire T/F - 5487542 Customer Ref - GAL457 Pd Ord :- HT11234 PO No: TYL. RP : N
16. Mr M W Cravens 12 Hoener Dale. Settle, Lincoln T/F - none, try email? Customer Ref - WCR Pd Ord :- none PO No: Use Name. RP : Y	Mr M W Cravens 12 Hoener Dale. Settle, Lincoln T/F - none, try email? Customer Ref - WCR Pd Ord :- none PO No: Use Name. RP : Y
17. Mr SN Rowe (Rowan?) Cathean House, Cathern Way, Howarth, Surrey T/F - 1543243 Customer Ref - SNR8 Pd Ord :- RT1-3178 PO No: SN/PO2. RP : N	Mr SN Rowe (Rowan?) Cathean House, Cathern Way Howarth, Surrey T/F - 1543243 Customer Ref - SNR8 Pd Ord :- RT1-3178 PO No: SN/PO2. RP : N
18. Ms U Palms (check this please) 547 marrick Road, Stainburn, Edinburgh. T/F - 4569889 (old?) Customer Ref - WUP44 Pd Ord :- PT61 PO No: UPA. RP : Y	Ms U Palms (check please) 547 marrick Road, Stainburn, Edinburgh. T/F - 4569889 (old) Customer Ref - WUP44 Pd Ord - PT61 PO No: UPA. RP : Y
19. ME Queen 136 Fell Bank. Millfield, Essex T/F - mob - 74519977 Customer Ref - n/a no order Prd Ord :- waiting PO No: Use name RP : Unknown	ME Queen 136 Fell Bank. Millfield, Essex T/F - mob - 74519977 Customer Ref - n/a order Prd Ord :- waiting PO No: Use name RP : Unknown

20. Mr FGF Park
    4 Main Unit 4, Leathhad
    Buiness Park,
    Stockwell, Brighton.
    T/F - none given
    Customer Ref - FGF1
    Pd Ord :- unknown ?
    PO No: FGF/PO.
    RP : Y

    Mr FGF Park
    4 Main Unit 4, Leathhad
    Buiness Park,
    Stckwell, Brighton.
    T/F - none given
    Customer Ref - FGF1
    Pd Ord :- unknown
    PO No: FGF/PO.
    RP : Y

21. Mrs T Damuns
    78 Jubilee Ave.
    Maynard Hill, Hull.
    T/F - 4569874
    Customer Ref - TDS12
    Pd Ord :- FGD7x4
    PO No: TDA.
    RP : Y

    Mrs T Damuns
    78 Jubilee Ave.
    Maynard Hull, Hill.
    T/F - 4569874
    Customer Ref - TDS12
    Pd Ord :- FGD7-4
    PO No: TDA.
    RP : Y

22. Mr G Craige
    Greenbank Cottage
    Waughs Bank.
    Braeside
    T/F - 3444536
    Customer Ref - WGC3
    Pd Ord :- JJ6x3
    POrder No: POV44
    RP : N

    Mr G Craige
    Greenbank Cottage
    Waughs Bank.
    Braeside
    T/F - 3444536
    Customer Ref - WGC3
    Pd Ord :- JJ6/3
    POrder No: PO44
    RP : N

23. Ms JJ Finchal
    Flat 2, Anick Hall.
    Bentfoot, Sheffiled
    T/F - 5658995
    Customer Ref - NEW1
    Pd Ord :- SW -432
    PO No: JJF.
    RP : Y

    Ms J.J. Finchal
    Flat 2, Anick Hall.
    Bentfoot, Sheffiled
    T/F - 5658995
    Customer Ref - NEW1
    Pd Ord :- SW -432
    PO No: JJF.
    RP : Y

24. Mr K Lynedale
    6 Brindles Road.
    Birkshaw, Enfield.
    T/F - n/a - use email
    Customer Ref - KLY
    Pd Ord :- TU7-9891
    PO No: KL/PO6.
    RP : N

    Mr K Lynedale
    6 Brindles Road.
    Birkshaw, Enfield.
    T/F - n/a - use email
    Customer Ref - KLY
    Pd Ord :- TU7-9891
    PO No: KL/PO6.
    RP : N

25. Q A Ronald
    4 Rutland Gdns.
    Leazes, Manchester
    T/F - mob:789987609
    Customer Ref - QAR
    Pd Ord :- 546-S60
    PO No: Use name.
    RP : Y

    Q A Ronald
    4 Rutland Gdns.
    Leazes, Manchester
    T/F - mob:78987609
    Customer Ref - QAR
    Pd Ord : 546-S60
    PO No: Use name.
    RP : Y

26. Mr T Elmet
    12 Eastland Walk
    Leyburn, Selkirk
    T/F - 565755 (fax)
    Customer Ref - TEL1
    Prod Ord :- 784-Q232
    PO No: n/a.
    RP : N

    Mr T Elmet
    12 Eastland Walk
    Leyburn, Selkirk
    T/F - 565755 (tel)
    Customer Ref - TEL1
    Prod Ord :- 784-Q232
    PO No: n/a.
    RP : N

27. CT Rushey
    Top Flat, 12 Raby Rd.
    Stonesdale, Halifax
    T/F - none
    Customer Ref - CTS4
    Pd Ord :- MG7-V8
    PO No: n/a.
    RP : Y

    CT Rushey
    Top Flat, 12 Raby Road.
    Stonesdale, Halifax
    T/F - none
    Customer Ref - CTS4
    Pd Ord :- MG7-V8
    PO No: n/a.
    RP : Y

28. Mr TF Lacy
    55 Crown Ave.
    Eastwood, Drummond.
    T/F - use email
    Customer Ref - TBC
    Pd Ord :- no order
    PO No: TFL.
    RP : Y

    Mr TF Lacy
    55 Crown Ave.
    Eastwood, Drummond.
    T/F - n/a email
    Customer Ref - TBC
    Pd Ord : no order
    PO No: TFL.
    RP : Y

29. Mrs Cromlech
    14 Rayner Rd.
    Shenstone, Wakefield
    T/F - 45698225
    Customer Ref - CRO
    Pd Ord :- 879-S56
    PO No: name as ref
    RP : Y

    Mrs Cromlech
    14 Rayner Rd.
    Shenstone, Wakefield
    T/F - 45698225
    Customer Ref - CRO
    Pd Ord :- 879-S56
    PO No: name as ref
    RP : Y

30. Mrs GT Linden	Mrs GT Linden
88 Mews House Road.	88 Mews House Road.
Wheatcroft, Bramley.	Wheatcroft, Bramly.
T/F - use email	T/F - use email
Customer Ref - GTL	Customer Ref - GTL
Pd Ord :- FG4-5x4	Pd Ord :- FG4-54
PO No: n/a.	PO No: n/a.
RP : N	RP : N

Answers: For each question, the number of elements that have been changed are: **1:** 1; **2:** 0; **3:** 3; **4:** 2; **5:** 2; **6:** 1; **7:** 2; **8:** 0; **9:** 2; **10:** 3; **11:** 1; **12:** 2; **13:** 3; **14:** 2; **15:** 2; **16:** 0; **17:** 0; **18:** 3; **19:** 1; **20:** 2; **21:** 3; **22:** 2; **23:** 2; **24:** 0; **25:** 2; **26:** 1; **27:** 1; **28:** 2; **29:** 0; **30:** 2.

Chapter 14

Personality Assessment Sample Tests

In This Chapter

▶ Perusing your personality

▶ Producing your personality profile

*T*he time has come with this chapter to delve deep into your psyche and unearth the 'real' you hiding underneath that cool exterior. Here, you open the lid on your personality.

The statements and questions I give you in this chapter have no right or wrong answers, or pass marks. Their purpose is to help draw up a description of your personality. You can't pass or fail! For this reason, they are more like personality questionnaires or assessments than personality tests, although most people refer to them as tests for convenience, as I do throughout this book.

This chapter gives you the chance to try out a couple of personality tests. The first test uses descriptive statements, and the second uses *adjectives* (words that describe you). In reality, both tests do the same thing (which is to measure and describe your personality), but I've included both because they are two of the most common formats.

Try to answer the questions from the point of view of how you see yourself, and not how you would *like to be* in an ideal world, or how you think other people see you. If you wonder where to find the answers, remember that no such thing as a correct answer exists in personality tests, so I can't provide a list of what the correct answers should be after each test! Instead, I tell you how to score and interpret your answers.

I provide a chart (see Figure 14–1) on which you can draw up your own personality profile, using the scoring instructions to help you. I suggest that you draw the profiles from both tests on the same profile chart, using different coloured pens, and look at how closely they match. They probably don't match exactly, because asking every question to completely capture how you'd behave in every possible situation is about as difficult as getting a pair of matching socks from the washing machine. To find out what uses recruiters have for personality profiles, refer to Chapter 9.

You, I, and everybody else are all flexible and adaptive creatures, with an astonishing capacity to adapt and survive in a continually changing environment, and this is reflected in your personality profile, which would vary a little every time you sat the test. This ability to change is the real beauty of being human.

Personality Tests

Full-length personality tests can contain 400 or more questions, with anything up to seven response options for each. These questions are a lot easier to answer than those in the ability test chapters. Many candidates find the personality test to be a welcome breather from the hectic pace of the recruitment process. Both tests in this chapter are based on those from a personality test I developed, and they relate to the 'Big Five' theory of personality (refer to Table 1–1 in Chapter 1). Looking at the 'scoring' section after each test enables you to see (in most cases!) how the content of the questions relates to measuring traits.

The very brief tests in this chapter are just to illustrate the nature of the questions you may face in a real-life situation, and the processes of scoring and drawing up a personality profile. This profile can never be completely accurate, so don't base any major career decisions upon it!

Long question format

In this long question format test, you need to answer the questions below, by circling the response that best describes how you feel in relation to each statement. The test is untimed – take as long as you need.

1. I get lonely on my own and prefer other people's company.

(a) Not like me   (b) A bit like me
(c) Quite like me   (d) Very like me

2. I tend to worry and things can prey on my mind.

(a) Not like me   (b) A bit like me
(c) Quite like me   (d) Very like me

3. I am more technical than artistic.

(a) Not like me   (b) A bit like me
(c) Quite like me   (d) Very like me

4. I'd rather be in charge than have others in charge of me.

(a) Not like me   (b) A bit like me
(c) Quite like me   (d) Very like me

5. I'd rather set and follow my own rules.

(a) Not like me   (b) A bit like me
(c) Quite like me   (d) Very like me

6. I don't see others as just acquaintances and try to be friends with the people I know.

(a) Not like me   (b) A bit like me
(c) Quite like me   (d) Very like me

7. I can get easily upset and it doesn't take much to annoy me.

(a) Not like me   (b) A bit like me
(c) Quite like me   (d) Very like me

8. I'm a 'no nonsense' practical sort of person.

(a) Not like me   (b) A bit like me
(c) Quite like me   (d) Very like me

9. I'll argue with people if I think I'm right.

(a) Not like me   (b) A bit like me
(c) Quite like me   (d) Very like me

10. I don't like taking risks.

(a) Not like me   (b) A bit like me
(c) Quite like me   (d) Very like me

11. I'm not that private a person and I tell people what's going on in my life.

(a) Not like me   (b) A bit like me
(c) Quite like me   (d) Very like me

12. I can feel unhappy, even when nothing particularly bad is going on.

(a) Not like me   (b) A bit like me
(c) Quite like me   (d) Very like me

13. I'm not really that sentimental by nature and I tend to stick to the facts.

(a) Not like me   (b) A bit like me
(c) Quite like me   (d) Very like me

14. I don't like other people telling me what to do.

(a) Not like me   (b) A bit like me
(c) Quite like me   (d) Very like me

15. I prefer things to be well planned and organised.

(a) Not like me   (b) A bit like me
(c) Quite like me   (d) Very like me

Long format scoring

Here's what you need to do to score your long format answers:

1. Score your responses using the following scale. Feel free to scribble all over this book (it is yours after all!)

Very like me   3 points

Quite like me   2 points

A bit like me   1 point

Not like me   0 points

Note: For questions 2, 7, and 12, reverse the scoring system like this:

Very like me   0 points

Quite like me   1 point

A bit like me   2 points

Not like me   3 points

2. Add together the scores from the following questions:

Sociable   Q1 + Q6 + Q11 =

Stability   Q2 + Q7 + Q12 =

Logical   Q3 + Q8 + Q13 =

Independent   Q4 + Q9 + Q14 =

Disciplined   Q5 + Q10 + Q15 =

3. Transfer your totals to the correct row of the personality profile chart (see Figure 14–1), marking where your score falls with an 'x'.

4. Join your x's together using straight lines. Well done, you've just drawn your own personality profile! However, before you start reading too much into your profile, make sure that you read the 'Interpreting Your Results' section later in the chapter.

Short question format

In this short question format test, you need to look at each word listed below. Circle the response beneath each statement that best describes how much the word describes you.

1. Friendly

(a) Like me   (b) Somewhat like me   (c) Not like me

2. Self-doubting

(a) Like me   (b) Somewhat like me   (c) Not like me

3. Practical

(a) Like me   (b) Somewhat like me   (c) Not like me

4. Assertive

(a) Like me   (b) Somewhat like me   (c) Not like me

5. Organised

(a) Like me   (b) Somewhat like me   (c) Not like me

6. Affable

(a) Like me   (b) Somewhat like me   (c) Not like me

7. Unhappy

(a) Like me   (b) Somewhat like me   (c) Not like me

8. Unsentimental

(a) Like me   (b) Somewhat like me   (c) Not like me

9. Competitive

(a) Like me   (b) Somewhat like me   (c) Not like me

10. Self-disciplined

(a) Like me   (b) Somewhat like me   (c) Not like me

11. Outgoing

(a) Like me   (b) Somewhat like me   (c) Not like me

12. Gloomy

(a) Like me   (b) Somewhat like me   (c) Not like me

13. Tough

(a) Like me   (b) Somewhat like me   (c) Not like me

14. Bossy

(a) Like me   (b) Somewhat like me   (c) Not like me

15. Careful

(a) Like me   (b) Somewhat like me   (c) Not like me

16. Affectionate

(a) Like me   (b) Somewhat like me   (c) Not like me

17. Apprehensive

(a) Like me   (b) Somewhat like me   (c) Not like me

18. Rational

(a) Like me   (b) Somewhat like me   (c) Not like me

19. Self-confident

(a) Like me   (b) Somewhat like me   (c) Not like me

20. Systematic

(a) Like me   (b) Somewhat like me   (c) Not like me

21. Likeable

(a) Like me   (b) Somewhat like me   (c) Not like me

22. Worrying

(a) Like me   (b) Somewhat like me   (c) Not like me

23. Thick-skinned

(a) Like me   (b) Somewhat like me   (c) Not like me

24. Forceful

(a) Like me   (b) Somewhat like me   (c) Not like me

25. Methodical

(a) Like me   (b) Somewhat like me   (c) Not like me

Short format scoring

Here's how to score your short format answers:

1. Score your responses using the following scale:

Like me	2 points
Somewhat like me	1 point
Not like me	0 points

Note: For questions 2, 7, 12, 17, and 22, reverse the scoring system like this:

Like me	0 points
Somewhat like me	1 point
Not like me	2 points

2. Add together the scores from the following questions:

Sociable	Q1 + Q6 + Q11 + Q16 + Q21=
Stability	Q2 + Q7 + Q12 + Q17 + Q22 =
Logical	Q3 + Q8 + Q13 + Q18 + Q23 =
Independent	Q4 + Q9 + Q14 + Q19 + Q24 =
Disciplined	Q5 + Q10 + Q15 + Q20 + Q25 =

3. Transfer your totals to the correct row of the personality profile chart (see Figure 14–1), marking where your score falls with an 'o'.

4. Join your o's together using straight lines. Well
done! You've completed your second personality
profile. Hopefully, this profile isn't too different
from the first.

Trait						Trait
Score	0–2	3–4	5	6–7	8–10	Score
Shy, reserved						Sociable, people-oriented
Calm, relaxed						Anxious
Sentimental						Logical, task-focussed
Group-oriented						Independent
Undisciplined						Disciplined
Score	0–2	3–4	5	6–7	8–10	Score
Trait						Trait

Figure 14–1: Your personality profile chart.

Interpreting Your Results

Personality is often seen as comprising five global factors
known as the *Big Five* (Chapter 9 tells you more about these
factors), and you can probably tell that the profile you've just
completed is designed to measure them.

Remember that these personality profiles are based on only
two brief example tests, and are only rough indications of
your preferences. You are the expert on your own personality,
not me! However, the tests do demonstrate two different ways
of measuring your personality.

From a practice point of view, how many questions a test has
doesn't matter. A test with 300 questions is no harder than
one with 30 questions – it just takes longer! I've deliberately
kept these tests brief, and have included them so that you
get a feel for the question style, and see how the results are
turned into a personality profile.

You can't compare yourself to a fully developed and researched *norm* group for the preceding two tests (see Chapter 1 for more info about norm groups). However, I've designed the questions so that you get a rough idea of where you are. Considering a score of 5 to be an average for most people may be useful. As I've said before though, don't give your profile too much credence.

Part IV
The Part of Tens

'Ok, I'll take your word for it that
you're happy with who you are.'

In this part . . .

This part of the book focuses on the two key areas that you're most likely to be concerned about.

In Chapter 15 I go through ten things to remember during your test to help you manage yourself. Chapter 16 suggests ten ways of keeping yourself calm, so that you can perform to your true potential.

If you need something to read in the hour before your test, make it this part.

Chapter 15

Ten Things to Remember for the Test Session

*Y*ou may have spent hours preparing and practising for your test, but your preparation can count for nothing if you don't manage yourself properly through the process.

I see candidates making the same mistakes time and time again. Here are my top ten tips for avoiding them.

Don't Be Late

Being late stresses you out, and makes you lose focus. Plan your arrival carefully, but don't be *too* early! Arriving half an hour early for a test doesn't bother administrators, but sitting alone in reception twiddling your thumbs for that long allows your mind to start dwelling on things.

Bring Your Own Kit

Make sure that you bring a watch, a couple of pens and pencils, a pencil sharpener, and a rubber to the test with you. Administrators aren't always well prepared, and having your own stuff with you means that you have one less thing to worry about when you arrive.

Look After Yourself

Make sure that you're comfortable and physically prepared before you start the test. Do go to the toilet, even if you feel you don't need to. Make sure that you have a drink to hand if you're allowed one during the test.

If you can, choose to sit somewhere out of direct sunlight and away from radiators (unless you feel cold!). You may be facing a couple of hours' worth of testing – a long time to be uncomfortable.

Take the Test Seriously

Even though the administrator may be friendly and informal, and treat you as an equal, don't lose sight of the fact that the test is a formal assessment. Your future employment may depend on it.

Treat the test as an exam. Keep your focus and effort going all the way through. Now is the time to give any competitive or ruthless streaks within you free rein.

Pay Attention to Instructions

During the administration instructions, concentrate on what you're being asked to do, in particular how you should make your responses.

Test administration procedures are carefully worked out and tested – on lots of trial subjects – to be as clear and concise as possible, so do precisely what you're asked.

Every instruction you receive is given for a very good reason. For example, if you're told to use a pencil, use a pencil. You may receive this instruction because you need a rubber to change your answers – very tricky if you've used a pen to mark your responses.

You can find more information about administrators and the instructions they give you in Chapter 2.

Ask Questions Before the Test Begins

Be sure that you know exactly what you have to do before starting a test. If you don't understand something in the test administration, ask for clarification. Don't worry how many people are there. Asking questions shows the recruiter that you've engaged with the process and are paying attention.

Don't worry about looking foolish if you pluck up the nerve to ask a question. You can guarantee that other candidates want to know the answer too. Asking questions can also trigger other candidates into asking about issues that you hadn't considered, but which may be useful to know about.

Make Sure That You Understand the Examples

The examples you receive at the start of a test are your last chance to get to grips with the question format. You're normally asked if you understand how the examples work, and if not they can be explained to you. Going back through the examples helps you out if you get stuck during a test, so if you don't understand them now, ask to go through them again before the actual test starts.

Know Your Limits

Make sure that you know how much time you're allowed for the test. This time should be explained to you during the administration process, but if not then be sure to ask. Also make sure that you know whether this time is a guide or a strict limit.

With an ability test, hearing that 'you have 20 minutes to complete the test' means that's all you get, and you're stopped bang on 20 minutes. With a personality test, if you're told that 'most people take about 30 minutes to complete the test', this is to give you an indication of how long the test may take you.

Use Your Time Well

Time passes more quickly during a test than you expect: 45 minutes can pass quickly; 20 minutes goes by in the blink of an eye. Wear a watch and keep a check on how you're progressing through the test.

If you're halfway through the allowed time and haven't made much progress through the test, you may need to work faster.

Keep Your Chin Up

Don't lose heart if you come across a few hard questions early in the test, or if you find you're progressing more slowly than you'd like.

Most ability tests have questions of varying degrees of difficulty. In a typical test, you come across some difficult questions, and some much easier questions. So, you can expect to be pushed hard.

You can't really tell just by looking whether a test is designed so that candidates can complete it all in the time allowed. So don't panic if you don't get to the end of the test with time to spare.

Chapter 16

Ten Calming Thoughts to Keep in Mind

● ●

In This Chapter

▶ Keeping things in perspective

▶ Focusing on the positives

▶ Accepting yourself for who and what you are

▶ Staying relaxed about the process

● ●

*'P*sychometric' and 'test' are two of the most feared words in the English language!

You aren't human if you don't get nervous about facing a test, and I bet you ask yourself the same anxious questions that candidates have always asked – *How will I do? Will I be okay? Will they want me for this job? What if I perform terribly?*

You need to feel relaxed on the day of your test so that you can perform as near to your optimum level as possible. A few nerves are fine – they keep you on your toes. By the time your test is about to start you're at a pretty high level of alertness. But if nerves or anxiety take over, your performance ends up well below what you know you're capable of.

You need to make sure that a few nerves don't turn into full-blown anxiety. So, here are a few snippets of advice to bear in mind, just to help you keep everything in perspective.

You Are Who You Are

A psychometric test isn't something that you can pass or fail – all that psychometric tests do is describe you. The testing process just allows you and the recruiter to get that description of yourself out into the open so that people can see the real you!

Your ability and personality are who you are – and you don't need to make any apology for that.

You're Not in the Last Chance Saloon

If your test results aren't as good as you'd hoped for or expected, all isn't necessarily lost. Other assessment tools are probably also being used as well that give you have a chance to show what you can do. Even if you're not successful in your application, other jobs are always out there.

If you're not well suited to the job you've applied for, that fact is generally a good thing to find out about.

Psychometric Tests Are Fair

Done properly, testing is a very fair selection method. You don't need to worry about being unfairly treated. Take comfort from the fact that the recruiter is using a test. Tests enable you to undergo a fairer assessment than if you faced only an unstructured interview.

Recruiters Should Be Well Trained

If the recruiter uses a test, the chances are that he's been trained properly, especially in larger and well-respected companies. The professional qualifications required to use tests are now well known in human resource circles and fewer and fewer people administer tests without them. Refer to Chapter 2 for advice on what to do if you feel your recruiter isn't up to scratch.

Nobody's Perfect

Psychometric tests aren't like exams where you can revise hard and score 100 per cent. Everyone has individual strengths and weaknesses. You can't expect to do brilliantly every time you're assessed.

Positivity Pays Off

Smile! Even if you don't feel optimistic, behaving in an upbeat, cheerful manner makes you feel more upbeat and cheerful. Stand on the balls of your feet, and not on your heels (the old stand up comedian's trick to help you engage with people).

Don't sit in stony silence when you arrive for your test. Talking to the receptionist, the recruiter, or the other candidates makes you feel better. Ignore any scare stories or attempts to wind you up from the other candidates. Your fellow candidates are all feeling the same as you, even if they don't say so.

You're Probably Better Than You Think

You're quite likely to do better in your test than you ever expected. You may just astonish yourself. For every three or four candidates I assess, I find one who had no idea he would do as well as he did in his tests.

Refer back to Chapter 3 for lots of tips on how to prepare, and maximise your chances of pleasantly surprising yourself!

Knowledge Doesn't Count

In ability and personality tests, knowledge and education don't give you that much of an edge. Even if you've not done any formal academic work for years – or ever – you're still on a level playing field with the other candidates.

People get better at tests with practice. The examples in this book give you the chance to practise taking psychometric tests. By working through these tests, you're already improving your chances!

You're Always Better Off After a Test

If you've never been tested before, taking your first psychometric test is a great opportunity (for free!) to discover what you're really good at, and what you need to work on.

In most cases, if the recruiter does his job properly, you receive feedback on your performance no matter how you perform. This feedback is very useful to help you identify your own development areas.

The worst you can expect is to get a detailed picture of where your strengths and weaknesses lie.

Tests Are Good Things!

Psychometric tests themselves are not bad things.

Remember that many people voluntarily and willingly put themselves through detailed psychometric assessment to help with their career development. The only difference between recruitment and development is the use to which the test results are put – the tests used are often identical.

Index